Timeline for Application/Admission to Medical School

Use this general guide to help prepare for the medical school application and admission process. Be sure to talk to your pre-health advisor to create a schedule that works best for you.

COLLEGE YEAR 1	• Talk with an academic advisor about selecting fall semester courses • Make an appointment with a pre-health advisor to introduce yourself, discuss the best way to sequence your classes and get acquainted with campus resources • Attend pre-health meetings on campus and make sure you are on email lists to get relevant updates and information • Seek opportunities to volunteer, shadow a doctor, and, if interested, identify research opportunities on your campus • Develop relationships with faculty, advisors, and mentors on your campus • Explore the AAMC's *Considering a Medical Career* resources (*www.aamc.org/students/considering*) • Identify summer volunteer, paid, research and leadership opportunities related to medicine • Apply to summer enrichment programs (*http://services.aamc.org/summerprograms/*) or research programs (*www.aamc.org/members/great/61052/great_summerlinks.html*) • Complete first year premedical coursework and other school-specific degree requirements
SUMMER FOLLOWING COLLEGE YEAR 1	• Work or volunteer for a position in the medical field; consider internships, research and leadership opportunities on campus or in your local community • If you're eligible, participate in summer enrichment or research programs • Take summer courses through a university if desired or necessary
COLLEGE YEAR 2	• Check-in with your pre-health advising office; attend all pre-health meetings, and make sure you're still on email lists to receive information and updates • Pursue meaningful clinical experience, medically-related activities, volunteer work research and/or leadership roles • Continue to develop relationships with faculty, advisors, and mentors on your campus • Apply for summer research, internship, or enrichment programs such as the Summer Medical and Dental Education Program (*www.smdep.org*) • Consider returning to your previous summer position, or apply for a new summer volunteer, paid or research position related to medicine • Complete second year premedical coursework and other school-specific degree requirements

SUMMER FOLLOWING COLLEGE YEAR 2	• Work or volunteer in the medical field; consider internships, research opportunities and leadership positions on campus or in your local community
	• Participate in summer enrichment, research, or internship programs
	• Take summer courses through a university if desired or necessary
	• Investigate:
	  o The medical school application process (*www.aamc.org/students/applying/*)
	  o Medical College Admission Test (MCAT®) (*www.aamc.org/mcat*)
	  o Fee Assistance Program (FAP) (*www.aamc.org/fap*)

COLLEGE YEAR 3	• By this time, you should have a well-established relationship with a pre-health advisor and should be actively participating in pre-health activities
	• Identify and pursue leadership opportunities within the pre-health organizations on your campus
	• Consider which faculty, advisors and mentors on your campus, with whom you've developed relationships, you'll approach to write letters of recommendation for your applications
	• Continue your participation in meaningful clinical experiences, other medically related activities, volunteer work, research and/or leadership roles on campus; if possible, consider taking on a more substantial role
	• Investigate:
	  o Medical schools in the U.S. and Canada (*https://services.aamc.org/30/msar/home*)
	  o *Minorities in Medicine* to get information on groups underrepresented in medicine (*www.aamc.org/students/minorities/*)
	• Meet with your pre-health advisor to:
	  o Strategize about your application timeline, whether it be for immediately following graduation or after one or more gap years
	  o Discuss your schedule for completing remaining premedical coursework and other school-specific degree requirements

...continued on next page

COLLEGE YEAR 3 *(continued)*	o Identify the best time for you to take the MCAT® exam; visit the MCAT web site to find the best options for test dates and locations (*www.aamc.org/mcat*) o Discuss letters of recommendation and committee premedical evaluation (if available) o Review your medical education options • If you're prepared and ready, register for and take the MCAT exam in spring • If you are considering a gap/bridge year, investigate a meaningful paid or volunteer medically-related experience to complete during that time • Familiarize yourself with medical school application services: o American Medical College Application Service (AMCAS®) (*www.aamc.org/students/applying/amcas/*) o Texas Medical and Dental Schools Application Service (TMDSAS) (*www.utsystem.edu/*) • Research medical school curricula and joint, dual, and combined-degree programs • Complete third year premedical coursework and other school-specific degree requirements
SUMMER FOLLOWING COLLEGE YEAR 3	• Continue your involvement with meaningful paid, volunteer, internship, medically related, research and leadership experiences • If applying to begin medical school following your senior year: o Complete AMCAS application o Work on secondary applications o Ask instructors, mentors, and advisors to write letters of recommendation for you • When you're prepared and ready, if you haven't taken the MCAT exam yet, or if you want to take the exam again, sign up to take the MCAT exam in the summer
COLLEGE YEAR 4	• You should be regularly consulting with your pre-health advisor to: o Discuss letters of recommendation and committee premedical evaluation (if available) o Review your medical education options, such as a post baccalaureate premedical program (*http://services.aamc.org/postbac/*) o Discuss the status of your applications and the admission process for schools to which you've applied • If applying for enrollment immediately following senior year: o Complete supplementary application materials for schools to which you've applied o Prepare for your interviews and campus visits at medical schools o Become familiar with *AAMC Recommendations for Medical School and M.D.-Ph.D. Admission Officers* (*https://www.aamc.org/students/applying/recommendations/admissionofficers/*) o Become familiar with *Applicant Responsibilities* (*www.aamc.org/students/applying/policies*) • Continue with your meaningful clinical experiences, other medically related activities, volunteer work, research and/or leadership experiences • When you're prepared and ready, if you have not previously taken the MCAT exam or want to retake the exam, sign up to take the MCAT exam in the spring • If applying for enrollment immediately following senior year: o Receive acceptances! o Make interim and final decisions about your medical school choice o Notify medical schools that you will not be attending on or before the deadline given o Ensure that all IRS and financial aid forms are completed and submitted as early as possible • Complete degree requirements and graduate
SUMMER FOLLOWING GRADUATION	• If enrolling immediately following senior year: o Purchase books and equipment and make appropriate living arrangements o Attend orientation programs and matriculate into medical school • If applying for enrollment following a gap/bridge year(s): o Complete AMCAS application o Work on secondary applications o Ask instructors, mentors, and advisors to write letters of recommendation for you
GAP/ BRIDGE YEAR(S)	• Seek meaningful employment, education and/or experience • Pay down credit card and/or undergraduate debt as much as possible • Continue to consult regularly with your pre-health advisor throughout the process • Complete supplementary application materials for schools to which you've applied • Interview and take campus tours at medical schools • Become familiar with *AAMC Recommendations for Medical School and M.D.-Ph.D. Admission Officers* (*https://www.aamc.org/students/applying/recommendations/admissionofficers/*) • Become familiar with *Applicant Responsibilities* (*www.aamc.org/students/applying/policies*)
ONCE ACCEPTED INTO MEDICAL SCHOOL	o Make interim and final decisions about medical school choice o Notify medical schools that you will not be attending on or before the deadline given o Ensure that all IRS and financial aid forms are completed and submitted as early as possible o Purchase books and equipment and make appropriate living arrangements o Attend orientation programs and matriculate into medical school

AAMC
Tomorrow's Doctors, Tomorrow's Cures®

MSAR®:
Getting Started

Medical School
Admission Requirements

*The Most Authoritative Guide
to Preparing for and Applying
to U.S. Medical Schools*

Association of
American Medical Colleges

MSAR: Getting Started, 2014–2015

AAMC Staff

MSAR® Guide Program Staff
Tami Levin,
Director, MSAR® and Aspiring Docs
Programs

Jennifer Kuzmik,
Web and MSAR® Content Specialist

Douglas Ortiz,
Director, Creative Services

Kudirat Momoh,
Senior Graphic Designer

Content Specialist
Geoffrey Young, Ph.D.,
Senior Director,
Student Affairs and Programs

Consultants
Kelly Begatto,
Program Director, AMCAS

Geoffrey Reddin,
Database Specialist

Lisa J. Jennings,
Senior Specialist,
Diversity Constituent Services

Jack Krakower, Ph.D.,
Senior Director, Med School Financial
and Administrative Affairs

Jodi Lubetsky, Ph.D.,
Manager, Science Policy

David A. Matthew, Ph.D.,
Senior Research Analyst,
Student and Applicant Studies

H. Collins Mikesell,
Senior Research Analyst,
Student and Applicant Studies

Karen Mitchell,
Senior Director,
Admissions Testing Services

Julie Gilbert,
Senior Education Debt Management
Specialist

Shelley Yerman,
Senior Specialist, Student Financial Aid

To order additional copies of this publication, please contact:

Association of American Medical Colleges
Publications Department
2450 N Street, NW
Washington, DC 20037
Phone: 202-828-0416
Fax: 202-828-1123
E-mail: *publications@aamc.org*
Web site*: www.aamc.org/publications*

Price: $15.00 for print edition,
plus shipping (single copy);
$12.00 for e-book/Kindle edition.

MSAR Kindle 2014-2015
978-1-57754-120-2

MSAR e-book 2014-2015
978-1-57754-121-9

MSAR: Getting Started 2014-2015
978-1-57754-122-6

Printed in the United States of America
Revised annually; new edition available in
early spring.

Group on Student Affairs (GSA) Steering Committee, 2012–2013

Chair
W. Scott Schroth, M.D., M.P.H.
Associate Dean for Administration
George Washington University
School of Medicine & Health Sciences

Chair Elect
Marc J. Kahn, M.D., M.B.A.
Senior Associate Dean for
Admissions & Student Affairs
Tulane University School of Medicine

Vice Chair
Robert L. Hernandez, M.D.
Associate Dean for Student Affairs
Florida International University
Herbert Wertheim College of Medicine

Immediate Past Chair
Patricia A. Barrier, M.D., M.P.H.
Senior Dean for Student Affairs
Mayo Clinic College of Medicine

Previous Past Chair
Maureen Garrity, Ph.D.
Associate Dean for Student Affairs
University of Colorado School of Medicine

Chair, Central Region
Wanda Lipscomb, Ph.D.
Associate Dean for Student Affairs
Michigan State University
College of Human Medicine

Chair, Southern Region
Kathleen Fallon, M.D.
Senior Associate Dean for Student Affairs
Texas A&M HSC - College of Medicine

Chair, Northeast Region
Adam Aponte, M.D., M.Sc, FAAP
Assistant Dean for Diversity & Inclusion
Hofstra North Shore - LIJ School of Medicine

Chair, Western Region
Edward P. Junkins, Jr., M.D., M.P.H.
University of Utah School of Medicine

Chair, Committee on Admissions
Gabriel Garcia, M.D.
Associate Dean of Medical School
Admissions
Stanford University School of Medicine

Chair, Committee on Diversity Affairs
Wanda Lipscomb, Ph.D.
Associate Dean for Student Affairs
Michigan State University
College of Human Medicine

Chair, Committee on Student Affairs
Thomas Koenig, M.D.
Associate Dean for Student Affairs
Johns Hopkins University School of Medicine

Chair Committee on Student Financial Assistance
Cheri Marks
Coordinator, Financial Aid and
Student Records
University of Missouri-Columbia
School of Medicine

Chair, Committee on Student Records
Rondel Frank, M.H.A.
Registrar
Tulane University School of Medicine

Council of Deans Liaison
Steven L. Berk, M.D.
Vice President for Medical Affairs and
Dean, School of Medicine
Texas Tech University Health Sciences Center
School of Medicine

Chair-Elect, Organization of Student Representatives
Ronnie Zeidan
Student
Medical College of Georgia at Georgia
Health Sciences University

National Association of Advisors for the Health Professions Liaison
Charles Hauck
Chief Health Professions Advisor
The University of Iowa

Association of American Medical Colleges

The Association of American Medical Colleges (AAMC) has as its purpose the advancement of medical education and the nation's health. In pursuing this purpose, the Association works with many national and international organizations, institutions, and individuals interested in strengthening the quality of medical education at all levels, searching for biomedical knowledge, and applying these tools to providing effective health care.

As an educational association representing members with similar purposes, the primary role of the AAMC is to assist those members by providing services at the national level that will facilitate the accomplishment of their missions. Such activities include collecting data and conducting studies on issues of major concern, evaluating the quality of educational programs through the accreditation process, providing consultation and technical assistance to institutions as needs are identified, synthesizing the opinions of an informed membership for consideration at the national level, and improving communication among those concerned with medical education and the nation's health. Other activities of the Association reflect the expressed concerns and priorities of the officers and governing bodies.

The Association of American Medical Colleges is a not-for-profit association representing all 141 accredited U.S. and 17 accredited Canadian medical schools; nearly 400 major teaching hospitals and health systems, including 51 Department of Veterans Affairs medical centers; and nearly 90 academic and scientific societies. Through these institutions and organizations, the AAMC represents 128,000 faculty members, 75,000 medical students, and 110,000 resident physicians.

In addition to the activities listed above, the AAMC is responsible for the Medical College Admission Test (MCAT®) and the American Medical College Application Service (AMCAS®) and provides detailed admissions information to the medical schools and to undergraduate premedical advisors.

Important Notice

The information in this book is based on the most recent data provided by member medical schools prior to publication at the request of the Association of American Medical Colleges (AAMC).

This material has been edited and in some instances condensed to meet space limitations. In compiling this edition, the AAMC made every reasonable effort to assure the accuracy and timeliness of the information, and, except where noted, the information was updated as of February 2013. All information contained herein, however, especially figures on tuition and expenses, is subject to change and is non-binding for medical schools listed or the AAMC. All medical schools listed in this edition, as with other educational institutions, are also subject to federal and state laws prohibiting discrimination on the basis of race, color, religion, sex, age, disability, or national origin. Such laws include Title VI of the Civil Rights Act of 1964, Title IX of the Education Amendments of 1972, Section 504 of the Rehabilitation Act of 1973, the Americans with Disabilities Act, and the Age Discrimination Act of 1975, as amended. For the most current and complete information regarding costs, official policies, procedures, and other matters, individual schools should be contacted.

In applying to U.S. or Canadian medical schools, applicants need not go through any commercial agencies. The AAMC does not endorse any organization or entity that purports to assist applicants to achieve admission to medical school other than undergraduate pre-medical advisors and medical school admissions officers.

AAMC Commitment to Diversity

Diversity within medical education and the physician workforce is essential to the health of the nation. The benefits of diversity in medicine will continue to increase as the nation ages, becomes more diverse along many dimensions, and experiences inequities in health care. The AAMC's commitment to diversity in medicine and biomedical research spans more than three decades and is demonstrated by ongoing leadership and engagement in activities that promote diversity through programs, advocacy, and research. This commitment has been reaffirmed in the publication *Learn, Serve, Lead: The Mission, Vision, and Strategic Priorities of the AAMC*, which states that the AAMC's mission is to serve and lead the academic medicine community to improve the health of all. To support its mission, AAMC's vision and that of its members is, in part, to establish "…a healthy nation and world in which… [t]he nation's medical students, biomedical graduate students, residents, fellows, faculty, and the health care workforce are diverse and culturally competent…." As a result, leading efforts to increase diversity in medicine is among the AAMC's nine strategic priorities.

To achieve this end, the AAMC works with its members to:

- advance diversity in academic medicine and biomedical research that fully embraces the diversity of the nation;

- generate and coordinate research, collect evidence, and disseminate studies pertinent to diversity in academic medicine and biomedical research;

- lead policy and advocacy efforts for diversity in academic medicine and biomedical research;

- direct pipeline programs and services across the education continuum to increase diversity in academic medicine and biomedical research;

- communicate the relationship of diversity in medicine and biomedical research to ameliorating disparities in health and health access outcomes; and

- supply resources and guidance to educators seeking to maximize the benefits of diversity across the medical education continuum.

Contents

CHAPTER 1:
So...You Want to be a Doctor

Contents

Tables & Charts

Maybe it was the great feeling you had from volunteering, or the profound concern stirred by a family member's illness that made you first think seriously about becoming a doctor. Or, perhaps it was the thrill you experienced solving a complex research problem that inspired you to dream about finding the next "big cure." Whatever reason led you to consider a career in medicine, you have come to the right place: the Medical School Admissions Requirements (MSAR®).

Published annually by the AAMC (Association of American Medical Colleges)—the national association representing all 141 accredited U.S. and 17 accredited Canadian medical schools—the MSAR® guides are the only medical school application resources authorized by medical schools themselves. The comprehensive MSAR Online resource will tell you about each school's focus, mission, and curriculum, as well as its entrance requirements and selection factors. The *MSAR: Getting Started* guidebook and ebook explains how medical schools increasingly are taking a holistic approach to admissions decisions by evaluating candidates' experiences and personal attributes in addition to their academic credentials and metrics, such as MCAT® exam scores.

On the MSAR Online Web site, you will find details about financial aid and costs, and see the degree of diversity represented by 2012 matriculants. And, in what I think is one of the MSAR Online's best features, you will see that diversity reflected in the number of accepted applicants at each school who took certain premed courses, performed community service, or worked in research or other medically related positions.

In other words, you will read about students who, only a few years ago, went through the same decision-making process you are undertaking now.

We have made a special effort to further "demystify" the medical school application and acceptance process. For example, the book provides a more detailed description of the American Medical College Application Service® (which you will use to apply to medical school) and includes a chapter on choosing the right school for you. We also have drawn from a wealth of data gathered by the AAMC and other sources to provide a more in-depth profile of today's medical students. Examples range from at what age these students decided to become a doctor, to the specialties they considered at the time of matriculation, to the ways they prepared for medical school.

Should you decide to apply to medical school, I think you will find it is an extraordinary time to be a doctor. You will be entering medicine at a time when the country needs your services most, given predicted physician shortages in coming years, and when national attention is focused like never before on the need to improve health care delivery. It is also a time when our profession is undergoing an exciting period of transformative change, with clinical care becoming increasingly patient-centered and team-based, biomedical research more technically sophisticated and collaborative, and medical education itself evolving into a continuum of lifelong learning.

Whatever career you decide to pursue, please accept my best wishes for success. And, if being a doctor is the path you choose, please know that the AAMC stands ready to help you. It would be a special pleasure for me if—during your education and training—our paths should cross and we have the opportunity to meet.

Darrell G. Kirch, M.D.
President and CEO, Association of American Medical Colleges

Dear Medical School Applicant,

Congratulations on your pursuit of a career in medicine! In so doing, you have embarked on a lifelong journey. As a physician, you will ascertain medical skills and expertise to provide healing and comfort to patients with a myriad of disease pathologies. Academically, you will be a life-long learner and participate in the development of advanced technologies and treatment regimens. Professionally, you will be an advocate, encourager, and leader of interdisciplinary and interprofessional healthcare teams. Personally, you will touch the lives of your patients and their families; and at the same time, your life will be touched as you share in their infirmities. Each aspect of a physician's lifestyle will be combined to improve the health and well-being of the communities you serve, locally and abroad.

The process of applying to medical school is overwhelming. Searching for the appropriate school that provides the opportunities you desire to meet your career goals is time-consuming, expensive, and challenging. To help demystify the process and guide you through the steps necessary to successfully complete the application process, the Association of American Medical Colleges (AAMC) has created this book to help you along the way. The Medical School Admission Requirements (MSAR®) guide will provide you with the most up-to-date information about U.S. and Canadian medical schools so that you can make a well-informed decision about how and where to pursue your medical studies.

As you navigate this process, you will find there is no one path to becoming a physician. Medical schools are searching for applicants with integrity, compassion, and altruistic ideals combined with a diverse set of experiences and backgrounds. In regards to preparation, Sir William Osler, a world renowned physician, told some of his students, "Live neither in the past nor in the future, but let each day absorb all your interest, energy and enthusiasm. The best preparation for tomorrow is to live today superbly well." If your goal is to become a physician, stay focused, become as informed as possible, and persevere.

As Chair of the AAMC Organization of Student Representatives (OSR), and on behalf of the 75,000 medical students and 110,000 resident physicians, we look forward to welcoming you into the profession as a future colleague. We hope you will join us as we commit ourselves to learn, serve, and lead in the healthcare of humanity.

Ronnie Zeidan
Fourth Year Medical Student
Medical College of Georgia at Georgia Health Sciences University
2012–2013 Chair, AAMC Organization of Student Representatives

CHAPTER 1:

So...You Want to be a Doctor

Maybe it was the day you won first place in the science fair. Maybe it was the time your family physician made a lifesaving call during your little brother's illness. Maybe it was the summer you volunteered in an underserved area and realized how the lack of access to healthcare impacted a community.

At some point, you just knew. You wanted to be a doctor.

But, as you also undoubtedly know, you now face a major step in the journey: getting into medical school. It involves everything from completing your undergraduate preparation to taking the MCAT® exam...from selecting appropriate schools to navigating the application process...from arranging for financing to performing well on the interview. Big challenges do indeed lie ahead.

But so, too, does the ultimate reward: a career in medicine.

When Did You Decide to Study Medicine?

Most of you knew early on that you wanted to be a doctor. According to an AAMC survey, half of all entering medical students made their decision to study medicine before they even started college:

- 20% before high school
- 29% during high school or before college
- 23% during first two years of college
- 11% during junior year of college
- 4% during senior year of college
- 11% after receiving bachelor's degree
- 2% after receiving advanced degree

Source: AAMC's 2012 Matriculating Student Questionnaire (MSQ)

An Exciting and Gratifying Career

It's something that many of you knew from an early age. In fact, a recent AAMC survey shows that almost half of all entering medical students had decided upon a medical career before they even set foot in undergraduate school—and one in five had made the decision before they even started high school.

Nowhere else can you find a career that offers as many opportunities to make a real difference in the lives of thousands of people.

You'll have job security, of course, knowing that your services will always be in demand. You'll earn an excellent living. You'll seldom experience the tedium of a nine-to-five desk job.

There's so much more than that, of course. As a doctor, you're likely to see new life come into the world, or provide comfort to those about to leave it. Or maybe you'll choose to help build the future of medicine by educating the next generation of physicians. Perhaps you'll dedicate yourself to discovering new cures for diseases that devastate millions of people and their families.

Whichever direction you follow, you will—either directly or indirectly—reduce or eliminate people's pain and suffering, improve their quality of life, and, provide invaluable service to your local community or the country as a whole.

How many careers can even come close?

Some of you were deeply influenced by your parents to pursue medicine. Others were intrigued by a science course. But the single strongest influence on the decision to study medicine, based on an AAMC survey, was a health-related work experience.

Some Influencing Factors Include:

- Health-related work experience
- Science course
- Challenge of medicine
- Parent(s)
- Physician
- Experience with illness/accident
- Health professions advisor

Source: AAMC's 2012 Matriculating Student Questionnaire (MSQ)

Dozens of Options from Which to Choose

The fact that you have so many options is another benefit of a career in medicine. From clinical practice to biomedical research, from public health to medical education—the choices are almost limitless. Beyond that, you'll also enjoy the flexibility that a medical career provides. If your interests change with time and experience, medicine—because of its emphasis on lifelong learning—will provide you with ample opportunity to refine your skills and reorient your practice. A number of possible career options are listed below:

- The satisfaction of long-term patient relationships is one attraction of **family medicine or internal medicine**, where the bulk of time is spent in direct contact with patients. Physicians in this area—which comes under the umbrella term of "primary care"—often care for entire families and enjoy the challenge that comes from treating a diverse population with varied backgrounds and conditions.

- Other physicians may prefer to pursue detailed knowledge about the intricacies of a single organ or system, such as that required of **cardiologists, ophthalmologists, dermatologists, and endocrinologists.**

- Interested in **scientific exploration** and the desire to **break new ground in medical knowledge?** Physicians with these interests are found in the nation's private and public laboratories and research institutions.

- Those with a commitment to social justice and an interest in fulfilling the health care needs of the underserved and disadvantaged can meet those challenges in **urban and rural clinics, in public health, or as medical missionaries.**

- Careers in **general surgery** often suit those with a desire to see immediate results of their interventions. **Plastic and reconstructive surgery** draws others with artistic skills and aesthetic interests.

- Those interested in mind-body interactions and the emotional lives of their patients might find a home in **neurology or psychiatry.**

- The fast pace of medicine draw some to work as **emergency physicians or trauma surgeons.**

- Others motivated in the interest of national defense may use their skills as **flight surgeons or in military medicine.**

- The **economic and public policy aspects of health care** guide some physicians to think-tanks and health-related organizations, as well as to serve in the legislative and executive branches of government.

- For those fascinated by the issues facing groups of patients with age-defined illnesses and problems—from the risks of infancy and early childhood to the challenges of older life—fulfillment can come in careers as **pediatricians and geriatricians**.

- Assisting patients in overcoming complex fertility and gestational problems is the hallmark of the specialists in **reproductive endocrinology and obstetrics and gynecology.**

- Those dedicated to reducing the incidence of birth defects and inherited diseases might find their calling in the field of **medical genetics.**

- The detection, prevention, and eradication of injury and disease draw people to the fields of **preventive medicine and epidemiology.**

Clearly, the possibilities in medicine are almost endless. No matter what your personal interests, skills, or needs may be, medicine encourages you to find your niche.

Entering medical students have a definite preference for the MSQ practice areas they plan to enter after graduation. The following list shows the percent of students who are considering the specialties listed below.

Specialty	Percent
Internal medicine	16.8
Pediatrics	13.9
Orthopedic Surgery	9.1
Emergency medicine	8.9
Family medicine	7.4
Obsterics and Gynecology	4.7
Neurology	4.7
Radiology	3.2
Dermatology	2.9
Anethesiology	3.3
Ophthalmology	2.3
Surgery	10.1
Neurological surgery	3.1

Source: AAMC's 2012 Matriculating Student Questionnaire (MSQ)

Career Intentions: Academic v. Clinical?

A relatively small—but not insignificant—percentage of matriculants plan to work in academia, and a larger percentage are undecided. Students' career intentions at the time they enter medical school are shown below.

	Percent
Full-time academic faculty (teaching and research)	9.3
Full-time clinical practice	62.1
Other	8.9
Undecided	19.7

Source: AAMC's 2012 Matriculating Student Questionnaire (MSQ)

How to Decide Which Path Is "Best"

Which path is right for you? With the ever-changing world of medicine and a myriad of options and practice settings, figuring out where you belong as a physician can be one of the hardest decisions of your career.

Fortunately, you won't have to make this decision alone.

Medical schools realize how daunting this decision can be. They have a program in place to help you assess your personal values and interests, identify specialty options, determine personal "fit," and make a well-informed choice about your career path. This program, called Careers in Medicine® (CiM) was developed by the Association of American Medical Colleges (AAMC) in collaboration with its 141 member medical schools, to guide you through the decision-making process.

The Careers in Medicine program is completely free-of-charge to students attending AAMC-member medical schools. For more information, go to *www.aamc.com/careersinmedicine*.

What About the Future?

As long as we're looking ahead, let's look way ahead. Five years. Ten years. Fifteen years. What will medicine look like then?

Recent Advances and Future Trends

One thing is for certain. The face of medicine changes continually*. Take a look back just a single generation, and you'll discover an abundance of fields that weren't even in the embryonic stage 25 years ago.

- An obvious example made its entrance in the early 1980s. Back then, a new—and fatal—illness was taking hold that nobody could identify. Now, though, it has a well-known name—**AIDS**—and infectious disease is currently a large medical subspecialty. As a result, significant advances have been made in extending the lives of those infected with **HIV**.

- Other advances are more recent. **Minimally invasive** surgery, in which surgeons carry out precise procedures with the assistance of a robot, is becoming increasingly popular. It is currently used for a variety of surgeries, including those involving the lungs, esophagus, prostate, uterus, and kidneys. Through robotic-assisted surgery, patients are likely to benefit from smaller incisions, lower risk of complications, shorter hospital stays, less pain, and a speedier recovery.

- What about the exciting advances in personalized medicine? A nonexistent career path for the previous generation, the technology in this field allows physicians to identify mutated genes and alert patients of their predisposition to a specific disease. (The next step—to actually treat disease with genes—is on the horizon. See section below.)

- Then there are more established fields that have evolved to take on new parameters. Take radiology, for example, which is no longer about just reading an X-ray. The radiologist can now do the actual surgery as part of **interventional radiology.**

* In the 1976–77 academic year, women comprised just 24.7 percent of all medical school matriculants. Compare that to 2012–2013, in which they made up almost half—or 46.4 percent—of the entering class.
Source: AAMC Data Book.

Even more exciting, though, is what lies ahead. Genetics therapy. Portable medical records. Distance surgery. Focused medication. And more.

- Right now, physicians can diagnose predisposition to certain illnesses by identifying mutated genes. Currently in the research and development stage is the next step— **gene therapy**—in which physicians will actually replace defective genes by giving patients copies of the correct gene (which, in turn, "overtakes" the mutant gene). Early tests have been especially favorable for cystic fibrosis, in which the correct CFTR gene is transported via a harmless virus or liposome.

- Similarly, research is underway in the field of **pharmogenetics**—in which a patient's treatment is tailored according to the specific genetic code in question. For example, if a patient's genes fit a certain type of cancer code, the physician will prescribe the "matching" pharmaceutical that has been developed to destroy them—and will know, rather than hope, that the treatment is likely to work. Most forms of focused medication care involve oncology, but studies are progressing in areas of cardiology, diabetes, psychiatric disorders, and more.

- Also in development is **focused preventive care**, which, using genetic diagnosis, identifies to a very specific degree how likely a patient is to develop a certain disease or condition—and then usurps that development before it has a chance to begin.

- Other advances will be administrative in nature: The days of hunting down medical records may come to an end. One possibility being explored is a **portable medical records** system, or a national online database of individual health records. Everyone will carry a smart card (or have a microchip inserted under his or her skin!), allowing physicians to access medical records. The benefit? Errors are reduced; files can no longer be lost; delays are minimized; and the experience of having repeated—i.e., unnecessary—tests is eliminated.

- And what about the robotics-assisted surgery we mentioned earlier? It provides the foundation for the next step forward—that of **distance surgery.** One day, surgeons will operate via a computerized system that will be located hundreds, even thousands, of miles away from patients. This, of course, opens up a "world" of possibilities and opportunities, in which specialists in one country can perform surgery on patients located in another.

Workforce Issues

Above all, know this: Whatever specialty you choose, your services as a physician will be needed—a need that will only increase as the years move forward.

According to the AAMC's Center for Workforce Studies, there will be 45,000 too few primary care physicians – and a shortage of 46,000 surgeons and medical specialists – in the next decade. The passage of health care reform, while setting in motion long-overdue efforts to insure an additional 32 million Americans, will increase the need for doctors and exacerbate a physician shortage driven by the rapid expansion of the number of Americans over age 65. Our doctors are getting older, too. Nearly one-third of all physicians will retire in the next decade just as more Americans need care. Continued demand for physicians and other medical professionals is obvious.

The graph to the left illustrates the growing physician shortages between now and 2020. Still, the shortage will be experienced unevenly, and some areas will feel the effect more strongly than others. With that in mind, you may wish to consider the trends as you think about the direction you'd like your career to take.

Chart 1-A

Projected Supply and Demand, Physicians, 2008–2020

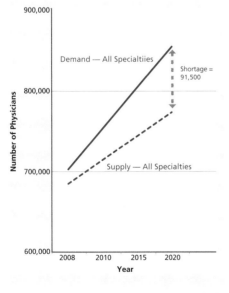

Source: AAMC Center for Workforce Studies, 2010.

- **Primary Care:** Although the nation is facing an overall shortage of physicians, many are particularly concerned about the growing deficit of primary care doctors. To encourage more U.S. medical school graduates to pursue a career in primary care, the government is exploring ways to more fairly value primary care efforts and lessen administrative burdens associated with general medicine. You might want to explore the rewards this specialty offers, including the satisfaction that comes from the delivery of comprehensive care and the continuity of patient relationships.

- **Underserved Areas:** In addition, the impact of this shortage is expected to be greatest on underserved areas—the urban and rural areas where health care is already scarce. If you choose to serve in a community designated as a Health Professional Shortage Area, you may be able to take advantage of a federal program—the National Health Services Corps—that offers scholarships and loan repayment. *(Learn more about this program in Chapter 11, How to Finance Your Medical Education.)*

A More Collaborative Approach

As Congress explores various scenarios as it moves toward instituting health care reform, one thing is all but certain: Given the projected shortage of physicians, we'll need to develop new models of health care delivery that make better and more efficient use of all health care professionals—not just doctors. That means you can expect to work within a more collaborative, "shared" environment, in which a team of health care providers—including physician's assistants and nurse practitioners, for example—work more in tandem. Exactly how that will play out is still in the development stages, but the goal is to create a more efficient system, increase patient satisfaction, and, ultimately, improve health outcomes.

This collaborative approach to health care delivery is instilled beginning in the early years of medical education. Read more about the use of small group discussions, problem-based learning, and other educational models in Chapter 3, From Here to There: The Medical Education Process.

The Immediate Steps that Lie Ahead

That's the long-range future, or at least what we anticipate it is likely to entail. Right now, though, you're undoubtedly more fixated on the short term—getting into medical school.

So what's the process like? What lies ahead?

First, let's be candid. Getting into medical school isn't easy. (But it's definitely doable, a fact to which the more than 76,000 students currently there can testify!) You'll need to prepare for and do well on the MCAT® exam, select appropriate schools to apply to complete the application process, write a personal statement, gather letters of evaluation, and the interview. And then you'll need to wait for notices of acceptance and make your final decision. On the other hand, if you're not accepted, you will need to evaluate options and determine a course of action.

All this we review in the following chapters.

But first, there are many steps you can take while still in college to make yourself a more attractive candidate to admissions committees. From taking the necessary courses, to working effectively with your pre-health advisor, to participating in extracurricular and volunteer activities that demonstrate your true interest in medicine, there's much you can do.

In the next chapter, we take a look at your undergraduate preparation.

Countdown to Medical School

The Timeline for Application and Admission, included at the front of this guide, outlines in detail the steps you should take at various stages during your undergraduate years. Major components include:

- Taking the MCAT® exam

- Selecting schools to which to apply

- Investigating medical school application services

- Completing the application process

- Learning about the financial aid system

- Applying for financial aid, if necessary

- Preparing a personal statement

- Participating in interviews

- Waiting for notification(s) of acceptance

- Making a final acceptance decision

CHAPTER 2:
Building a Strong Foundation: Your Undergraduate Years

Your path to the M.D. degree begins well before you set foot on a medical school campus.

In reality, it starts during your undergraduate years—a time during which you'll build a foundation that will not only make you a strong candidate to medical school, but ultimately an effective physician, as well.

As a college student planning to pursue the study of medicine, you have much to accomplish. You'll need to master general academic skills, select a major and fulfill its requirements, complete all necessary premedical courses, and, ideally, pursue advanced coursework in areas of special interest. But there's more to your undergraduate years than intellectual development alone. You'll also want to participate in a variety of extracurricular activities, and cultivate the personal traits expected of a physician.

And finally, you'll want to seek out someone to advise you. Although there are a number of people who can be invaluable—a professor, a current medical student, a physician, your parents—you'll certainly want to establish a relationship with a pre-health advisor or find a medical mentor in your community.

These areas combined—academic preparation, the nurturing of desirable personal attributes, participation in extracurricular activities, and appropriate guidance—will help ready you for entry to medical school.

Some Ways Students Prepare for Medical School

College students take advantage of a wide variety of programs to prepare for a career in medicine or science. The following shows the percentage of students who participated in:

Program	Percent
Volunteered or worked in the health care field	92.7
MCAT® preparation course (university-based or private)*	61.3
Laboratory research apprenticeship	57.2
Summer academic enrichment	12.4
Post-baccalaureate program to complete premedical requirements	9.4
Post-baccalaureate program to strengthen academic skills	6.8

*This figure is comprised of all preparation programs, including no or low-cost university-provided preparation courses.
Source: AAMC's 2012 Matriculating Student Questionnaire (MSQ)

Academic Preparation

Much of your preparation for medical school comes in the form of academic groundwork and development, which encompasses your major field of study, the mastery of specific scientific principles, and advanced coursework. Let's take a look at each of these a bit further.

Choice of Major

Contrary to what many college students believe, there is no such thing as the "best" major for those bound for medical school. **In fact, no medical school requires a specific major of its applicants.** That's because admissions committee members know that students develop the essential skills of acquiring and synthesizing information through a wide variety of academic disciplines and therefore should be free to select whichever majors they find interesting and challenging.

Even so, many premedical students choose to major in a scientific discipline. If that's the direction you're heading, and you're doing so because you are fascinated by science and believe that such a major will be the foundation for a variety of career options, great. If you're doing so because you believe it will enhance your chances for admission, think again. Admissions committee welcome students whose intellectual curiosity leads them to a wide variety of disciplines.

Table 2-A

Subjects Required or Recommended by 10 or More U.S. Medical Schools

Required/Recommended Subject	# of Schools
Biochemistry	28
Biology	101
Biology/Zoology	33
Calculus	13
College Mathematics	38
English	90
Humanities	14
Inorganic (General) Chemistry	127
Organic Chemistry	128
Physics	124
Social Sciences	12

N = 141. For premedical coursework required by the specific medical schools in which you are interested, please see the MSAR Online.

And no…you won't necessarily be at a disadvantage if you choose to major in English, for example, rather than biology. Using just one measure, those of MCAT® scores, you may be surprised to learn that there is very little difference in median total scores among those who major in the humanities, social sciences, and biological sciences.

The Official Guide to the MCAT Exam®, a guidebook available for purchase at *www.aamc.org/officialmcatguide*, includes a chart that provides the median MCAT® scores of applicants by undergraduate major. There you will see that the total median score for humanities majors, biology majors, and social sciences majors were 30, 28 and 29, respectively. This attests to the fact that students from any major, as long as they have the basic science preparation, are equally prepared for acceptance to medical school.

Scientific Preparation

Still, medical schools recognize the importance of a strong foundation in the natural sciences—biology, chemistry, and physics—and mathematics, and most schools have established minimum course requirements for admission. These courses usually represent about one-third of the credit hours needed for degree completion (leaving room for applicants to pursue a broad spectrum of college majors, as mentioned on the left). In particular, medical schools expect that their entering students will have mastered basic scientific principles by successfully completing one academic year (two semesters or three quarters) of biology and physics and one academic year each of general chemistry and organic chemistry, and including adequate laboratory experiences. Increasingly, biochemistry is strongly recommended by schools.

While only a few medical schools require applicants to complete a specific course in mathematics, all schools appreciate that mathematical competence provides a strong foundation for understanding basic sciences. A working knowledge of statistics helps students fully grasp medical literature, and familiarity with computers is valuable, as well. Many medical schools therefore recommend coursework in mathematics, statistics, and computer science in addition to the science courses named above. The table to the left gives an overview of the most common courses required by medical schools.

AP, IB, and CLEP Courses

Students intending to apply college credit earned through **Advanced Placement (AP), International Baccalaureate (IB), and College Level Examination Placement (CLEP)** to meet premedical requirements should be aware that some medical schools have requirements involving the use of such credit. Please review the MSAR® Online and the web sites of medical schools you're interested in for more information.

Competencies vs. Courses

Finally, for those of you reading this in the early years of college (or even in high school), we'd like to draw your attention to the fact that some medical schools may one day define their prerequisites by competencies—rather than courses. This comes about because, as a study undertaken by the Howard Hughes Medical Institute (HHMI) and the AAMC points out, the scientific knowledge medical schools seek in their applicants can be obtained in a variety of courses as opposed to specific ones. (In other words, a student might be able to master chemistry principles in a zoology class.)

Advanced Coursework

Although upper-level science coursework may not be required by medical schools, successfully completing advanced courses demonstrates science proficiencies and strengthens your preparation for medical school. However, taking science courses that duplicate basic content is not recommended. Practicing physicians often suggest that premedical students take advantage of what might be their final opportunity for study in non-science areas (such as music, art, history, and literature) they find of interest. Beyond that, medical schools encourage honors courses, independent study, and research work by premedical students. Activities such as these demonstrate in-depth scholarly exploration and the presence of lifelong learning skills that are essential to a career in the medicine.

Into the Future: Competency-Based Prerequisites

The Scientific Foundations for Future Physicians report (conducted by the AAMC-HHMI Scientific Foundation for Future Physicians committee) proposes scientific competencies for future medical school graduates and for undergraduate students who want to pursue a career in medicine. Competencies entering medical students should demonstrate include:

- both the knowledge of and ability to apply basic principles of mathematics and statistics, physics, chemistry, biochemistry, and biology to human health and disease;

- the ability to demonstrate observational and analytical skills; and

- the ability to apply those skills and principles to biological situations.

You may download a copy of this report, free-of-charge, at *www.aamc.org/scientificfoundations.*

Personal Attributes

As we mentioned in this chapter's introduction, academic and scientific accomplishments alone are not sufficient for a student's entry into medical school. While intellectual capacity is obviously important to success as a physician, so too are other attributes—those that portend the ability to develop and maintain effective relationships with patients, work collaboratively with other team members, act ethically and compassionately, and in many other ways master the "art" of medicine.

An AAMC publication entitled *Learning Objectives for Medical Student Education: Guidelines for Medical Schools* describes the personal attributes required of a physician. While making note of the fact that graduating medical students must, of course, be knowledgeable about medicine and skillful in its application, the publication also emphasizes how vital it is for students to:

- Make ethical decisions;

- Act with compassion, respect, honesty, and integrity;

- Work collaboratively with team members;

- Advocate on behalf of one's patients;

- Be sensitive to potential conflicts of interest;

- Be able to recognize one's own limits;

- Be dedicated to continuously improving one's knowledge and abilities;

- Appreciate the complex nonbiological determinants of poor health;

- Be aware of community and public health issues;

- Be able to identify risk factors for disease;

- Be committed to early identification and treatment of diseases;

- Accept responsibility for making scientifically based medical decisions; and

- Be willing to advocate for the care of the underserved.

A number of these attributes are developed not only in medical school, but may be nurtured throughout the college years, as well (and, as you will see in Chapter 7, are among the attributes that admissions officers seek when deciding whom to admit to their programs). You will have an abundance of opportunities to foster many of these qualities through your interactions with friends, classmates, and faculty…in the classroom, dining hall, and dorm… on sports teams, in school clubs, and during summer or part-time jobs.

Extracurricular Activities Related to Medicine

Your undergraduate years offer wonderful opportunities to become involved in a wide range of extracurricular activities, and certainly at least a few of them should involve the medical field. Experience in a health care setting; caring for an ill or elderly family member; participating in basic or clinical research efforts; working as an emergency medical technician; "shadowing" a physician; providing support to people in a rape crisis center, emergency room, or social service agency—these types of activities are recommended to those considering a career in medicine.

These pursuits provide you with the chance to learn more about the medical profession— and yourself. You will, for example, be able to:

- Explore different interests,

- Test out your natural inclinations to one or more endeavors,

- Come to better understand the nature of medical practice and the daily demands placed upon physicians,

- Assess your ability to communicate and empathize with people from different backgrounds and cultures, and

- Evaluate your willingness to put others' needs before your own.

While this self-analysis can help you decide if a career in medicine is an appropriate choice for you, your involvement with clinical or research activities might help admissions committees determine where your interests lie and demonstrate to them that you have explored various aspects of the medical field. We say *might*, though—rather than *will*— because admissions committees evaluate your experiences using at least three different criteria, and a greater value is assigned to certain types of pursuits than others.

Specifically, admissions committees look at the length of time you've invested, the depth of the experience, and lessons learned—in relation to any particular activity—so that a day-long blood drive or one-time-only shadowing experience is less enlightening than semester or year-long commitments. By the same token, active participation in an activity is viewed as more instructive than a passive one (such as observation). Most important, though, admissions committees want to know what students learned from their experiences, and you should therefore be prepared to address these kinds of questions about your community, clinical, or research experiences in your application materials (which we will discuss in Chapter 6).

Be Wary of the Checklist Approach

Do **not** approach your extracurricular activities with the idea of "checking off" a wide range and number of pursuits in order to impress the admissions committee. Three or four in-depth experiences from which you gained valuable lessons are far more significant—and telling—to admissions officers than dozens of short-term involvements.

Pre-Health Advisors

Fortunately, you're not on your own when it comes to preparing for medical school. You have valuable resources available to you—some of which are likely available right on your college campus: your pre-health advisor.

Depending on the individual school, pre-health advisors function on either a full- or part-time basis, and may be faculty members (often in the science department), staff members in the office of an academic dean or in the career center, directors of an advising office for pre-professional students, or a physician in part-time practice. Advisors belong to organizations such as the National Association of Advisors for the Health Professions (NAAHP, *www.naahp.org*) that assist them in their work—and help them to help you. If your school does not have a pre-health advisor available to you, the National Association of Advisors for the Health Professions, Inc. (NAAHP) has members who volunteer to help those who do not have access to an adviser. See the NAAHP's web site for more details (*www.naahp.org*). You can always reach out to medical school admissions personnel if you have specific questions about admission requirements or policies. Be sure to first check the medical school's Web site to see if the information is available there.

Services Provided

The support provided by pre-health advisors varies according to a number of factors. Generally speaking, though, services fall into five categories:

- **Academics.** Advisors are well informed about premedical coursework on their campuses and about developing suitable academic programs for premedical students. They collaborate with campus academic staff in designing study, reading skill, and test preparation workshops, and in offering tutoring programs, as well as inform their students of regional and national programs likely to be of interest.

- **Clinical and research experiences.** In working with advisory groups composed of college and medical school teaching and research faculty and community clinicians, advisors help identify part-time jobs, volunteer positions, and opportunities for independent study credit in local laboratories and offices.

- **Advising and support.** Advisors help students pursue realistic goals and maximize their potential, both meeting with them individually and providing group opportunities for students to meet with one another. Advisors often establish peer advising and mentoring programs, and are particularly sensitive to the needs of students who are members of a group currently underrepresented in medicine or are the first in their family to attend college.

- **Assistance to student organizations.** Advisors coordinate the activities of local and national organizations that serve premed students by planning programs, identifying funding sources, and arranging for campus visits from admissions and financial aid officers.

- **Sharing resources.** Well aware of the need by students for timely and pertinent information, advisors disseminate publications and other resources from relevant organizations, including the AAMC and the NAAHP. In addition, advisors provide computer access to web-based content on health careers programs and educational financing; distribute information about local regional, national, and international research and service opportunities; and stock a library of publications related to medical school and medical education.

Please contact your school's advisor to discuss the availability of these services.

The Pre-Health Committee Letter of Recommendation

There's another vital service that pre-health advisors offer their students (and often their alumni) that we haven't yet mentioned: the pre-health committee letter of recommendation.

This is usually a composite letter written on behalf of a medical school applicant by the college or university's pre-health committee. It presents an overview of the student's academic strengths, exposures to health care and medical research environments, contributions to the campus and community, and personal attributes such as maturity and altruism. In addition, the letter may address any extenuating circumstances that may have resulted in deficits in the student's performance during a course or semester, provide perspective on challenges the student may have encountered, and explain school-specific courses and programs in which the student has participated.

Some undergraduate institutions do not provide composite letters of evaluation but instead collect individual letters throughout the student's enrollment. Then, at the appropriate time, they distribute the letters to the medical schools where the student has applied.

Pre-Health Advisors: A Wide Range of Guidance

There are many instances in which a pre-health advisor may assist you.
These include helping you:

- Identify courses that satisfy premedical requirements;

- Determine a sequence for completing those courses;

- Find tutorial assistance, if needed;

- Plan academic schedules to accommodate both premedical coursework and other educational objectives, such as a study program abroad, a dual major, or a senior honors thesis;

- Locate volunteer or paid clinical and research experience;

- Strengthen your medical school application;

- Prepare for interviews and standardized tests;

- Arrange for letters of evaluation and recommendation; and

- Determine the most appropriate career paths based on individual strengths, values, and life goals.

Special Programs

Finally, we'd like to draw your attention to the following two programs that may be of interest (depending on where you fall in the education process):

- ***Combined Baccalaureate/M.D. Programs***
  If you're reading this book during the latter stages of high school, you might want to explore a combined B.S./M.D. program, offered at about a quarter of U.S. medical schools. Graduates of these programs, which range in length from six to nine years, receive both a bachelor's degree from the undergraduate institution and an M.D. from the medical school. For more details and a list of participating schools, please see Chapter 12 as well as the individual Baccalaureate/M.D. program profiles in the MSAR Online.

- **_Post-Baccalaureate Programs_**

  Perhaps, though, you're at a different stage along the educational continuum and have already graduated from college. If your major was something other than science, it's quite possible that you'll need to pursue additional coursework before applying to medical school. Post-baccalaureate programs, offered at colleges and universities across the country and ranging from formal one- or two-year programs to information part-time programs. These programs are available to help applicants who may need to strengthen their knowledge in the sciences, complete required premedical coursework, career changers, and those who may need academic enhancement. A searchable database of these programs can be found at _http://services.aamc.org/postbac._ You can also locate medical schools that have post-baccalaureate programs using the search features in the MSAR Online.

CHAPTER 3:
From Here to There: The Medical Education Process

What lies on the journey between the day you earn your college diploma and the day you're licensed as a fully certified physician? What steps must you successfully navigate before you are deemed a competent doctor, ready to function independently in your chosen field?

You probably already know the answer: Four years of medical school, a residency program lasting anywhere from three to eight years (or more, on occasion), and passing scores on the three USMLE step exams administered at various stages along the way.

But that's only the short version. There's more to the discussion than that—much more. How has the medical education process changed in recent years—both in terms of teaching methods and the topics you'll be taught? Which technological innovations are being used to train students? How does medical education today differ from that of a generation ago?

We take a look at these questions, and others, in the material that follows.

Straight to Medical School from College…or Not?

If a year or more has passed since you graduated from college, you're not alone. Almost half of matriculating medical students—50.9 percent—indicated in a recent AAMC survey that there was a "gap" between college and medical school of at least twelve months.

Source: AAMC's 2012 Matriculating Student Questionnaire (MSQ)

Undergraduate Medical Education: An Overview of the Medical School Years

At the core, all U.S. and Canadian medical schools have the same purpose—to educate their students in both the art and science of medicine, provide them with clinical experience, and, ultimately, prepare them to enter a three- to eight-year-long residency program (otherwise referred to as "graduate medical education"). That is why every school follows the same basic program—requiring students to acquire a basic foundation in the medical sciences, apply this knowledge to diseases and treatments, and master clinical skills through a series of "rotations."

That doesn't mean that a medical school…is a medical school…is a medical school. Far from it. Each school establishes its own curriculum and course format, so that, for example, a particular class required by one institution is an elective course in another. Even when medical schools seem to require identical courses, the content within them may differ, so that some of the material covered in immunology in one school, for instance, is presented in pathology in another. (The sequence in which courses are taken—and the very method by which the content is taught—may differ, as well.) Beyond that, the processes by which students are graded also vary from school to school, with some institutions following a pass/fail system, others an honors/pass/fail system, and still others a letter grading system.

But we're not saying that "anything goes," either, when it comes to medical schools. To the contrary, they must meet very exacting standards to earn (and maintain) accreditation, as established by the Liaison Committee on Medical Education (LCME). The LCME, cosponsored* by the AAMC and the American Medical Association, is the authority that accredits programs of medical schools that grant the M.D. degree in the United States, and reviews and approves curricula, organization, and student performance.

Beyond that required by the standards of accreditation, there are other strong parallels among medical schools. Speaking in very simplistic terms—and recognizing there is significant overlap between what has traditionally been referred to as "pre-clinical" and "clinical" years—the general structure of the overall programs follow a similar path: Students concentrate their efforts on the scientific underpinnings of medicine during the first two years, and on applying and refining that knowledge during a series of rotations during the second two years.

A Word about "Pre-Clinical" vs. "Clinical" Years

It's been traditional to view the first half of medical school as "pre-clinical" years and the second half as the "clinical" years. In one way, that's largely correct, but in another… well, not so much.

That's because there is an increasing overlap in content between these two stages of medical education. It is quite common, for example, for a student to have some clinical exposure in the first year of medical school. Similarly, during the so-called clinical years, students refine their understanding of underlying medical concepts and knowledge. It is important, therefore, to recognize that "pre-clinical" and "clinical" content can—and does—intersect at any stage in the medical school experience.

Building a Foundation of Knowledge

In almost all cases, you'll begin your medical school studies by learning how the human body is supposed to work—both in terms of structure and function. The focus will then shift to abnormal conditions and diseases, methods of diagnosis, and treatment options.

- *Normal Structure and Function*

  How does the healthy body work? That's what you'll be studying right out of the starting gate, and your courses will be many—and varied. Typically, your "basic" classes will include gross and microscopic anatomy, physiology, biochemistry, behavioral sciences, and neurology.

- *Abnormalities, Diagnostics, and Treatment*

  After you've learned what "healthy" looks like (and acts like), the focus of your coursework will shift—again, both in terms of structure and function. You'll study the full range of diseases and atypical conditions, methods by which diagnoses are made, and therapeutic principles and treatments. It is at this stage that you'll have classes in immunology, pathology, and pharmacology.

- *Other Topics*

  You'll be exposed to a wide variety of other topics. These will range from nutrition, to medical ethics, to genetics…from laboratory medicine, to substance abuse, to geriatrics. Health care delivery systems. Human values. Research. Preventive medicine. Human sexuality. Community health. The fact is that the subjects taught at medical schools are as varied, and potentially as numerous, as are the institutions themselves.

*Accreditation by the LCME is required for schools to receive federal grants and to participate in federal loan programs. In addition, eligibility of U.S. students to take the United States Medical Licensing Exam (USMLE)—a discussion of which appears in "Licensure and Certification: Ready to Function Independently" later in this chapter—requires LCME accreditation of their school. All medical schools listed in this guide are accredited by the LCME.

And that's just part of the picture. There's much more to "building a foundation" than mastering the scientific basis of medicine. During this period of your medical education, you will also learn the basics of interviewing and obtaining historical data from patients, conducting physical exams, interpreting laboratory findings, and considering diagnostic treatment and alternatives—in effect, readying yourself for the clinical rotations that follow in the latter half of medical school.

Finally, keep in mind that it's not all science—or even application of science (such as that required to interpret lab results and figure out a course of treatment). Medical schools recognize that physicians practice in a social environment—one in which effective team-building, collaborative, and communications skills are necessary. As a result, the very way in which students learn, and are taught, has evolved in recent years. (We discuss this in more depth in the section on the next page—the *"Changing Face of Medical Education."*

Acquiring "Hands-On" Experience through Clerkships

A major component of your undergraduate medical education, typically occurring in the third and fourth years, will be a series of required clinical clerkships or "rotations." These clerkships usually last from four to 12 weeks each, and provide students with first-hand experience in working with both patients and their families, and in both inpatient and outpatient settings.

While the pattern, length, and number of rotations differ from school to school, core clinical training usually includes clerkships in internal medicine, family medicine, obstetrics/gynecology, pediatrics, psychiatry, and surgery. Beyond that, and depending on your specific school's requirements, your program may also include clerkships in primary care and neurology, for example, or require participation in a community or rural program.

- ### What You'll Do
  During a clerkship, you'll be assigned to an outpatient clinic or inpatient hospital unit where you will assume responsibility for "working-up" a number of patients each week—collecting relevant data and information from them—and presenting findings to a faculty member. Beyond that, you'll participate in the ongoing care of patients, either during hospitalizations or through the course of outpatient treatment, and, when appropriate, interact not only with the patients themselves, but with their families, as well.

- ### And What You'll Learn
  There's no substitute, as you know, for "hands-on" experience—and plenty of it. During the course of your clerkships, you'll learn to apply basic science knowledge and clinical skills in diagnosing and treating patients' illnesses and injuries and will become adept interacting with patients (and their families) as you provide information, answer questions, and prepare them for the likely outcome. At the same time, you'll become effective working with all members of the health care team, whether at the bedside, during inpatient team discussions ("rounds"), or in case-based lectures and small-group discussions.

Electives

Medical schools, just like colleges, each have their own requirements—the courses and clerkships you must take to graduate.

But, also just like college, you'll enjoy an opportunity to explore special interests by way of electives. Offered in basic, behavioral, and clinical sciences, as well as in basic and clinical research, electives are usually available during your final year of medical school (although you might be able to take them at other times). They may be completed on your own campus, at other medical schools through a "visiting student program," through federal and state agencies, in international settings, and service organizations.

The Changing Face of Medical Education

Some of you may have heard of Abraham Flexner, who wrote a groundbreaking report on medical education 100 years ago. Although the basics of his 1910 model have survived to the present day—mainly, a four-year program affiliated with a university*—he never intended his model to serve for more than a generation. He knew, after all, that he could not predict the future.

Time has certainly proven him correct.

There is no way that Flexner could have anticipated the shifting demographics, technological advances, and evolving teaching techniques of the late 20th century and the first decade of the 21st century. You, on the other hand, will experience first-hand the reforms taking place in medical education—both in terms of what you'll learn, and how you'll learn it. Your courses may range from cultural diversity to health care financing, and you'll benefit from educational developments such as computer-aided instruction, virtual patients, and human patient simulation. It's an exciting time to be a medical student.

What You'll Learn

You're going to have to wield a scalpel in anatomy class early on in medical school, just as students in your parents' and grandparents' generations did 30 and 60 years ago. Certain things stay the same. That type of effort aside, though, there are many significant changes in medical education content, and schools are continually revising their curricula to reflect advances in science, breakthroughs in medicine, and changes in society. For example:

- Consider the demographic shift we'll experience as the baby boomers age. By 2030, the population of those over age 65 is expected to have doubled, and physicians will spend an increasing amount of time treating age-related problems such as Alzheimer's, heart failure, pulmonary disease, and bone disorders. As a result, most medical schools now include courses on geriatrics, palliative care, pain management, and complementary medicine, and other similar age-based material, in their curricula.

- Issues such as health literacy, nutrition, drug abuse, and family violence are important components of medical education. Because many of these and other health problems are related to culture and lifestyle, medical schools haves increasingly focused efforts on areas such as disease prevention, health promotion, and cultural diversity.

- Medical schools are placing an increasingly important emphasis on helping their students develop effective communications, allowing them to interact successfully with a diverse group of patients. Rather than being "left to chance," you'll be directly taught to assess family, lifestyle, and socioeconomic factors that may influence your patients' behavior, or affect their care.

Then, of course, there are the advancements in science and medicine themselves. (As researchers make breakthroughs in genetics diagnoses and treatments, for instance, that new knowledge is incorporated into the medical school program.) There are also expanded courses on medical ethics, examining some of the dilemmas physicians may face amid the advent of new technology; classes on financial decision making, in which students are taught to weigh the likely costs and benefits of various treatments; and sessions on evidence-based medicine and patient quality, providing students with the informational and tools they will need to deliver the best possible care.

The topics described here are only an overview of some possibilities. The specific courses you'll take as a medical student will vary depending on the school.

At the time of Flexner's report, many medical schools were small trade schools unaffiliated with a university, and a degree was awarded after only two years of study.

And How You'll Learn It

Do you have an image of sitting in a large lecture hall, surrounded by hundreds of your peers? While you'll certainly experience that aspect of medical school, that method of teaching is being replaced (to a significant degree) by other techniques. Here are a few of the most widespread methods:

- The traditional lecture-based approach is increasingly giving way to student-centered, small-group instruction—similar to the "case study" teaching method common in both law and business schools. In your case, you're likely to be assigned to small groups of students—overseen by a faculty member—in which you will focus on specific clinical problems. The aim here is to instill medical knowledge and skill as well as help you build the communications and collaboration skills you'll need as a resident, and, ultimately, as a fully licensed physician.

- Fast-moving technological advances have certainly affected the medical school education program. You'll probably use a computerized patient mannequin (or "whole body simulator") to apply the basic sciences you've mastered to a clinical context and refine your diagnostic skills. These simulators, which are easily customized to replicate a wide range of situations, are currently part of the curriculum in most medical schools.

- Another way medical schools employ new technology is with computer-aided instruction and "virtual" patients. Here, you'll apply newfound knowledge and skills via interactive web-based (or software) programs that simulate complex cases.

To learn more about the specific teaching methods of the medical school(s) in which you are interested, please see the applicable school listing in the MSAR Online (www.aamc.org/msar).

Choosing a Specialty and Applying for Residency

Required courses. Clerkships. Electives. There's a lot occupying your time and energy as you advance through medical school. Along with all that, you undoubtedly will give a lot of thought about the career path you'd like to pursue, exploring various options and researching different possibilities.

Although, it is during the final stages of your third year and your final year, some real decisions must be made. It is at this stage that you'll choose a specialty and begin applying to residency programs (the portion of your education that follows graduation from medical school). How will you make your selection, and how will you get in?

Choosing a Specialty

You really should begin exploring specialty options in your second year of medical school, and there's much to think about. You'll want to consider the nature of the work, training and residency requirements, lifestyle and salary factors, characteristics of physicians in the specialty, issues facing professionals in that particular field, and, of course, your own interests, values, and skills.

Where to begin your explorations? You will, of course, seek out the guidance of your advisors, such as the student affairs dean or clinical faculty as you investigate your options, and your school will likely offer various workshops and presentations to help you with your decision. In addition, and as we mentioned in the first chapter of this guide, you will probably have access to the Careers in Medicine® (CiM) program sponsored by the Association of American Medical Colleges (AAMC). This largely web-based program—which is available free-of-charge to students attending AAMC member medical schools—contains detailed information and interactive tools to help you work through the specialty choice process.

Included in this program are:

- specialty descriptions;

- residency and training requirements;

- Match data;

- workforce statistics;

- compensation; and

- links to more than 1,000 specialty associations, journals, and publications.

Registration is required for access to the CiM program. For more information, go to www.aamc.org/careersinmedicine.

Getting In

Once you've decided on a specialty, there's more to it than simply shooting off an e-mail to the director of a residency program and letting him or her know of your interest (as we're sure you already suspect). Rather, you must compete for a position. Much like the application process to medical school, you'll complete an application, craft a personal statement, submit letters of evaluation, and go through interviews. This undertaking is usually facilitated through an application service such as the AAMC's **Electronic Residency Application Service** (ERAS®), which transmits all related documentation via the Internet.

Applying is just the half of it, though, you've also got to be accepted by (or "matched" with) a residency program. This pairing comes about through the **National Resident Matching Program** (NRMP®) by which students' preferences for specific residency programs are compared with the preferences of residency program directors for specific applicants. The Match Results are released during the third week in March. The third Friday in March—more familiarly known as "Match Day"—is met with a great deal of anticipation as 17,000 medical school seniors learn where they will spend the next several years of their training.*

Graduate Medical Education (GME): The Residency Program

Once you've graduated from medical school, you can claim title to that hard-earned M.D. (or D.O., for graduates of osteopathic schools). But although much of the work is done—and people now call you "doctor"—the journey is far from over. In actuality, you're a "doctor-in-training," and your next phase is that of graduate medical education. The residency program awaits.

We won't get into the details of postgraduate work here, as we imagine that right now you're more interested in getting into medical school—and that you plan to worry about your residency program later. In a nutshell, though, the primary purpose of these programs is to provide medical school graduates (such as you, one day) with the skills and knowledge they need to become competent, independent physicians. Ranging in length from three to eight years, and sometimes more, their completion is necessary for board certification.

Because of their very nature, residency programs are conducted primarily in clinical settings—hospitals, outpatient clinics, community health centers, and physicians' offices, for example—and require residents (or "house officers" as they're sometimes known) to participate fully in patient diagnoses and treatment. When your time comes, you'll work under the supervision of physician faculty as you develop experience in your chosen

These 17,000 students are the graduates of medical schools that grant the M.D. In addition, 15,000 graduates of osteopathic (those granting the D.O.), Canadian, and international medical schools also compete for residency program assignments through the NRMP. To learn more about ERAS and NRMP, go to www.aamc.org/eras and www.nrmp.org.

U.S. Residents by Specialty	
Specialty	**# of Residents**
Allergy and Immunology	289
Anesthesiology	5,483
Colon and Rectal Surgery	81
Dermatology	1,180
Emergency Medicine	5,329
Family Medicine	9,743
Hospice and Palliative Medicine	117
Internal Medicine	22,500
Medical Genetics	85
Neurological Surgery	1,192
Neurology	2,008
Nuclear Medicine	132
Obstetrics and Gynecology	4,945
Ophthalmology	1,326
Orthopedic Surgery	3,470
Otolaryngology	1,457
Pain Medicine	270
Pathology-Anatomic and Clinical	2,327
Pediatrics	8,318
Physical Medicine and Rehabilitation	1,240
Plastic Surgery	323
Plastic Surgery-Integrated*	389
Preventive Medicine	265
Psychiatry	4,864
Radiation Oncology	644
Radiology-Diagnostic	4,533
Sleep Medicine	113
Surgery-General	7,833
Thoracic Surgery	219
Thoracic Surgery-Integrated*	38
Urology	1,104

Source: AAMC Data Book, 2013, for the 2011–12 academic year

* Integrated programs differ from subspecialty programs in that they include core surgical education.

The most popular subspecialties in internal medicine include:
- Cardio-vascular disease (2,427)
- Gastroenterology (1,371)
- Hematology and Oncology (1,480)
- Pulmonary disease and critical care medicine (1,379)
- Nephrology (918)

specialty, become proficient with both common and uncommon illnesses and conditions, attend conferences, teach less experienced colleagues, and, in general, adjust to the demands of medical practice.

Finally, just as medical schools vary, so too do residency programs. Depending on the area you choose to pursue, you might complete a preliminary year of broad clinical training before focusing on the specialty, as is common in anesthesiology, dermatology, psychiatry, and radiology. In other areas, such as family medicine and pediatrics, you'll enter the specialty track directly. (Your medical school advisor, and programs such as Careers in Medicine®, will present you with full information as you approach this stage of your medical education.)

Residency will be a demanding time, no doubt, but rewarding as well. Many physicians look back on their residency years as ones providing invaluable lessons that they carry with them to this day.

Inter-professional Education

When it comes to caring for patients, remember…you're not in this alone.

Rather, the delivery of medical care is a "team-based" effort that often includes not only doctors, but nurses, pharmacists, physical therapists, and other health care providers, as well. Because of that, it's absolutely vital that practitioners from all disciplines become familiar with one another's roles, perspectives, and even language and communication styles in order to be able to collaborate effectively and efficiently.

And medical educators want to help you develop that knowledge and ability. Your medical education therefore is likely to involve some form of "inter-professional education" in which you will share learning resources, work as a unit, or participate in other activities that encourage interaction among various categories of health care providers. In such a way, you—and they—will become more adept and successful working as a team, and, ultimately, be able to deliver a higher quality of care to patients.

Licensure and Certification: Ready to Function Independently

There's something else you'll need to do before you can be licensed as a physician: You've got to meet the standards of the **National Board of Medical Examiners** (NBME) and the Federation of State Medical Boards (FSMB). Together, these two bodies cosponsor the United States Medical Licensing Examination (USMLE), a three-step exam given at various stages of the medical education process.

So, along with documenting that you've completed the necessary educational and training programs for your specialty, you must also get passing scores on the USMLE. It is administered in stages as follows:

- **Step 1:** Usually taken at the end of your second year of medical school, Step 1 tests whether you understand and can apply sciences basic to the practice of medicine. Its focus is on principles and systems of health, disease, and methods of therapy.

- **Step 2:** Many medical schools require you to take (and pass!) Step 2 prior to graduation. It's actually two tests in one—the first evaluating your clinical knowledge (CK) and the second your clinical skills (CS). Basically, Step 2 assesses your ability to provide patient care *under supervision*.

- **Step 3:** After you've completed the first year of your residency program, you're eligible for Step 3—the concluding test that determines your readiness to apply your medical knowledge and clinical skills without supervision, with an emphasis on patient management in ambulatory settings.

Examples of Training Requirements for Specialty Board Certification

Specialty	Years Required
Anesthesiology	4
Emergency Medicine	3
Family Practice	3
Internal Medicine	3
OB/GYN	4
Pathology	3 to 4
Pediatrics	3
Psychiatry	4
Radiology	5
Surgery	5
Surgical subspecialties	6 or 7

Source: AAMC's Careers in Medicine Program

Plans for Certification in a Specialty

When asked if they planned to become certified in a specialty, medical school graduates answered:

Yes	83.2%
No	5.1%
Undecided	11.8%

Source: AAMC's 2012 Graduation Questionnaire (GQ)

It is the final assessment of your ability to assume independent responsibility for delivering medical care.

Upon completion of the appropriate educational and training programs, and achievement on the USMLE, you've done it. You are ready to apply for licensure in any of the 50 states, 10 provinces, 3 territories or the District of Columbia.

But…there's one additional step: certification. While it's not required for medical practice—as is licensure from a state or provincial medical board—certification in a specialty is strongly encouraged. Physicians apply voluntarily for this additional credential, which is granted by the American Board of Medical Specialties (ABMS) and involves a comprehensive examination. (Those who have satisfied all ABMS requirements are certified and are known as "diplomates" of the specialty board.) More than 75 percent of licensed physicians in the United States have been certified by one of the specialty boards, and interest remains high among the current cohort of new doctors. Almost 9 in 10 medical school graduates plan to become certified in a medical specialty.

Continuing Medical Education: The Practice of Lifelong Learning

Finally, medical education is a lifelong process, providing you with the opportunity to learn new skills and stay current with exciting and innovative developments.

The fast pace of change in medicine makes continuing education essential, and most states require participation in accredited continuing medical education (CME) activities. Physicians therefore participate in CME programs throughout their careers, ensuring they stay up-to-date with the rapid advancements in their specialties and maintain their clinical competence. Offered by medical schools, teaching hospitals, and professional organizations, these CME programs are reviewed by the **Accreditation Council for Continuing Medical Education** (ACCME) to ensure that high standards are achieved and upheld.

Continuing medical education reflects a commitment to lifelong learning that is a hallmark of the medical profession. For those of you interested in what your CME efforts will entail, go to *www.accme.org*.

CHAPTER 4:
All About the MCAT® Exam

One of our MCAT staffers overheard a couple of college seniors commiserating with one another about the test. After about 20 minutes of nonstop talk about various review courses, prep books, and practice options, one student stopped mid-sentence, looked at the other, and asked, "Why do they DO this to us?" The other student shook her head and shrugged in empathy, but we know the answer:

Because the MCAT exam does its job.

MCAT® Essentials: A Must-Read!

To be sure that you get the most complete and up-to-date information about the MCAT® exam, it is crucial that you read **MCAT® Essentials** (posted online at *www.aamc.org/mcat*) prior to registration.

The Role of the Exam

Simply put, the MCAT® exam helps admissions officers identify which students are likely to succeed in medical school. It does that by spotting those students who not only have a basic knowledge of science—which provides the foundation necessary in the early years of medical school—but also those with strong critical thinking and skills.

One can argue that college grades do essentially the same thing. But because an "A" in one school is not necessarily equivalent to an "A" in another, admissions officers do not have a "standard measure" against which to evaluate students. The MCAT exam fills that void.

It's no surprise, then, that when admissions officers look at MCAT scores in conjunction with grades—as opposed to grades alone—their ability to predict who will be successful in medical school increases by as much as 50 percent (using first- and second-year medical school grades as a benchmark). As a result, virtually every medical school in the United States, and many in Canada, requires applicants to submit recent MCAT scores.

Your MCAT Score: One of Many Selection Factors

It's important to recognize that admissions officers consider MCAT results in concert with many other selection factors—including those related to your experience and personal attributes—when making their decisions. See Chapter 7 to learn more about the various ways in which admissions officers evaluate medical school applicants.

How the Exam Is Structured

It's a pretty sure bet that you're no stranger to the concept of standardized testing. Starting in elementary school, and continuing on through your college admission exam (be it the SAT™ or ACT®), you've had lots of experience with multiple-choice questions taken in a controlled, timed environment.

Exam Structure

Specialty	# of items	Time
Physical Sciences	52	70 minutes
Verbal Reasoning	40	60 minutes
Biological Sciences	52	70 minutes
Optional (unscored) Trial Section	32	45 minutes

There are optional breaks of 10 minutes each between sections.

The MCAT® exam follows the same basic format. In this case, it's a computer-based test that lasts approximately five hours and consists of three scored multiple-choice sections—that of Physical Sciences, Biological Sciences, and Verbal Reasoning—and one optional unscored multiple-choice "Trial Section". Let's take a closer look:

- *Physical Sciences (PS)*

  The PS section covers general chemistry and physics via a total of 52 questions—39 of which are based on passages, as well as 13 "free-standing," independent questions. For this section, you will be tested on your capacity to interpret data presented in graphs and tables, your knowledge of basic physical sciences concepts and principles, and your ability to solve problems using that knowledge as a foundation.

- *Verbal Reasoning (VR)*

  The VR section evaluates your ability to understand, evaluate, and apply information and arguments presented in writing. The section consists of seven passages, each of which is about 600 words long, taken from the humanities, social sciences, and natural sciences. Each passage-based set consists of five to seven questions that assess your ability to extrapolate information from the accompanying passage. In total, there are 40 questions in this section.

- *Biological Sciences (BS)*

  The format of the BS section, which covers biology and organic chemistry, is identical to that of the PS section. It too has 52 questions, 39 passage-based and 13 independent. Like the PS section, it also tests your problem-solving ability and scientific knowledge (but in this instance based on biological sciences).

- *Trial Section*

  This is a voluntary and unscored section at the end of the exam that asks you to test out questions for a future version of the MCAT exam. If you chose to participate, you will be administered 32 questions in either: biochemistry, biology, chemistry, and physics or in psychology, sociology, and biology. Your answers will not contribute to your MCAT scores.

  Examinees demonstrating good faith effort on the Trial Section will receive:

  - $30 Gift Card e-mailed to you within 3-4 weeks.

  - Feedback on your performance that will allow you to compare yourself to others who participated in the Trial Section.

MCAT Scores

There are four scores associated with the MCAT exam, one for each of the three scored sections, and a "composite" (or total) score that presents the results for those three sections in the aggregate. The following is a quick overview:

- Each of the three scored multiple-choice sections (PS, VR, and BS) is scored individually from a low of 1 to a high of 15.

- In addition to the three scores, you will also receive a score representing the total of your three multiple-choice sections. If, for example, you received a 9-10-11, your total score would be reported as 30.

- Scores for the writing sample section, which is no longer being administered, will not be reported for tests taken in 2013 (and beyond), but they will continue to be reported for examinees who took the exam prior to 2013.

Comparing Your Score to Other Applicants and Acceptees, in General

For more information about how your scores compare to others (and how likely you are to be accepted to any medical school based on your scores and other selection factors), see Chapter 10 on Applicant and Acceptee Data or *www.aamc.org/data/facts*.

Comparing Your Score to Those Accepted by a Specific Medical School

You're likely to want to know even more—namely, how your scores compare to those accepted by the specific medical school(s) in which you're interested. For that information, view individual school profiles on the MSAR Online website: *www.aamc.org/msar.*

MCAT® Web Site

The Official MCAT® web site. Your first stop should be the MCAT® web site (*www.aamc.org/mcat*) where you will find a wealth of information. Included there, and available free of charge, are such materials as the MCAT® Essentials (required reading), a "Preparing for the MCAT Exam" section, and FAQs.

The Official Guide to the MCAT® Exam

You can get even more detailed information from this affordable 400-page guidebook (*www.aamc.org/officialmcatguide*), which includes more than 140 practice questions taken from real exams, tips to arrive at the correct answer, thoroughly explained solutions, step-by-step registration instructions, and extensive data on both applicants and acceptees.

Official Practice Tests from the AAMC

Also available are eight practice tests—with items from retired exams—that include solutions for each item, automated scoring and customizable feedback, and test assistance features such as the ability to highlight and search the passage text. **One of the practice tests is available free-of-charge at *www.e-mcat.com*.**

If you'd like to learn more about the scoring process itself, including how scores are "equated" across test forms and the myth of the "curve," you'll find a full discussion included in The Official Guide to the MCAT® Exam, available for purchase online: www.aamc.org/officialmcatguide.

Preparing for the Exam

While there is no one way to prepare for the MCAT exam, making sure you give yourself adequate time to prepare is critical. The amount of time you will need really depends on you. Have you completed all of the coursework that is associated with MCAT content? Do you feel confident in all content areas? Are there some content topics or skills that you feel require more in-depth study or practice? Are you comfortable with the online testing format?

You may also find it useful to break down the studying into manageable chunks, realizing that you can't tackle everything at once. This will also help give you a sense of the amount of time you will need so you can prepare at a comfortable pace. The best study plans are those that are tailored to an individual's needs.

7 Steps for Studying with the Official MCAT Prep Resources

1. Discover what topics may be covered and what skills will be tested on the exam with *content outlines*.

2. Get an introduction to the exam with *The Official Guide for the MCAT® Exam*.

3. Complete free *e-MCAT Practice Test 3* to get a baseline score.

4. Find out how *The Official MCAT® Self-Assessment Package* can help you; select Tutorials to view the videos.

5. *Consider buying a self-assessment* to learn your strengths and weaknesses in MCAT content.

6. Study by targeting your weaknesses and reinforcing your strengths.

7. Complete additional *e-MCAT Practice Tests* to monitor your progress.

Test Dates, Registration, and Fees

The MCAT® exam is administered more than two dozen times each year from January through September. (Specific dates are listed on the **MCAT® Exam Schedule**, posted on the MCAT® web site at *www.aamc.org/mcat*.) While the AAMC selects exam dates to ensure that scores are available to meet most medical school application deadlines, we recommend that you check the specific scheduling requirements of the school(s) of your choice, provided in the provided in MSAR Online school profiles. Once you've determined the date you prefer, you can find the registration schedule for that particular exam session on the **MCAT® Registration Deadline & Score Release Schedule**, also posted online.

After you have read the MCAT® Essentials (*www.aamc.org/mcat*), you can register for the exam—a process available online through the MCAT® web site. There will be a fee of $270 for each exam you take, a payment that covers both the cost of the test itself as well as distribution of your scores. If you register late, make changes to your registration, and/or test at an international site, there will be additional charges.

As a general rule, you should plan on taking the MCAT® exam 12 to 18 months prior to your expected entry into medical school—but not before you've completed basic coursework in general biology, inorganic chemistry, organic chemistry, and general physics. Many medical schools prefer that applicants take the MCAT® exam in the spring because of the short time between the availability of late summer scores and school application deadlines. (Taking the exam in the spring also allows time for students to retake the test later in the summer, if necessary). For more guidance, please see your pre-health advisor.

Testing with Accommodations

The AAMC supports the policies of the federal government and will provide accommodations to students whose disabilities—or other conditions—necessitate an adjustment to the test or testing environment, pending review and approval by the MCAT® Office of Accommodated Testing Services. Information about the process by which accommodations are requested (and the documentation that must accompany the request) is available at *www.aamc.org/mcat*.

Score Reporting

The time between the date of your exam and the day you find out how you did can seem like an eternity. In reality, though, scores will be reported through the MCAT® program's computerized Testing History Report System (THx) approximately 30 days after each exam. Through this program, located at *www.aamc.org/mcat*, you can check your scores and print your own official score report.

Of course, you're not the only one who's interested in finding out how you did. The medical schools to which you've applied (or will apply) want to know, as well. How then do admissions committees learn of their applicants' scores?

- ***Automatic Score Release to AMCAS:***

  The good news is that, in most cases, it's all automatic—and no action is required on your part. The American Medical College Application Service, or AMCAS® automatically releases your scores via the THx for all scores that date from April 2003 (which is probably your situation). For those of you who have scores prior to April 2003, you can use the THx system to make selected scores part of your current AMCAS® application.

- ***Score Release to Non-AMCAS® Schools:***

  For the 2012 entering classes, all but 7 of the 141 U.S. medical schools are part of the AMCAS® program. In the event you're applying to a non-AMCAS® institution, you can use the THx system to select those recipients.

The various options and procedures available through the THx system are explained in detail when you log into the system.

What's AMCAS®?

AMCAS® is a nonprofit, centralized application processing service in which most U.S. medical schools take part, and the process by which you will manage your application (to participating institutions). Through this system, scores are submitted to each school you've designated. For more information, please see Chapter 6, in which we discuss the AMCAS® application process in detail.

Retaking the Exam

If you're not happy with your performance on the MCAT® exam, you have the option to take it again. But it's a tough decision. Many medical schools average the scores from all tests taken—or consider only the last take—so that if you do worse the second time around, you may have actually weakened your position.

There are times when a retake is well worth considering. Perhaps you discovered that your coursework or study didn't cover the topics as thoroughly as you needed. Or there's a large discrepancy between your grade in a subject and your score on a particular section. Or maybe you simply didn't feel well the day of the exam. In all these cases, your pre-health advisor may be of great help, and we recommend you discuss the issue with him or her.

If you decide to retake the exam, please bear in mind that it may be taken a maximum of three times during each calendar year. Registration procedures for retaking the exam are identical to those for initial testing.

The MCAT® exam is administered and scored by the MCAT® Program Office at the direction of the AAMC. Information about the exam's content, organization, scoring system, accommodations process, and more, is available at www.aamc.org/mcat.

MCAT 2015

The MCAT is changing in 2015 for examinees applying to medical school in 2016. The new exam will have four sections all of which will be scored:

- Biological and Biochemical Foundations of Living Systems
- Chemical and Physical Foundations of Biological Systems
- Psychological, Social, and Biological Foundations of Behavior
- Critical Analysis and Reasoning Skills

Go to *www.aamc.org/mcat2015* for more details.

CHAPTER 5:
Choosing the School That's Right for You

No doubt you have many questions about the medical school application process. What forms will I need to complete? What are the logistics involved? What type of supporting documentation must I get? What's the timing of it all? How much will it cost me?

We address all that in the next chapter. For now, though, you've got an even bigger question to consider, and that's because the initial stage of the application process isn't really a "how" at all.

It's a "where." You first need to figure out to which school (or schools) you should apply. It's a question that is answered by looking not only at various medical schools, but at yourself, as well.

Because you're not searching merely for a school you can "get into." You're searching for the best possible fit.

Studentes Weigh a Host of Selection Factors

There's much to take into account when choosing schools. Among the factors medical students consider in making their ultimate selection as to which school to attend are:

- Interviews/meetings with administrators, faculty, and current students
- Advice of parents
- Advice of medical school graduates
- Advice of family physician
- Research reputation and opportunities
- Community-based experience and opportunities
- Geographic location
- School's teaching methods
- Program of elective courses
- Faculty mentorship
- Ability of school to place students in particular residency programs

Source: AAMC's 2012 Matriculating Student Questionnaire (MSQ)

The Overall Mission of the School

If you've seen one medical school...you've seen one medical school.

That's the standard way of saying that medical schools differ from one another. And many of these differences are pretty obvious. Some schools are located in the East; some in the West. Some are private; others, public. Some have a large entering class; others, small. And, as we explained in Chapter 3, medical schools vary in the content of their courses, in the way they teach, and even in the way they grade students.

These are all factors you'll want to consider as you narrow your selection, and we touch upon them in the pages that follow. But the differences go even deeper, and at a very core level: medical schools have diverse missions and priorities. Because of those distinctions, what's significant to one school may be of only moderate importance to another, and these goals naturally carry into the selection process.

To figure out where to apply, then, requires that you become aware not only of the differences among schools, but that you also analyze yourself—your skills, experiences, career goals, and so forth—to identify the most appropriate matches. Take, for instance, an institution that places a strong emphasis on primary care. Is that the career path you intend to follow? If so, and especially if you can demonstrate your interest through extensive experience related to that area, you become a more attractive candidate on that basis alone.

That's one example. Other schools may be actively seeking students from specific geographic or rural areas. Others may be looking for students with a high potential for a research career. Still others may want to increase the number of doctors who plan to practice in their state (this last goal is often found among public institutions). The differing missions among schools will be reflected in their admissions policies and standards.

If you need help with this self-analysis, think back to the various experiences you've had over the years. The ones you found especially rewarding or inspirational are likely to correlate to a specific area of interest, and, by extension, a career goal.

- Did you volunteer two summers for a clinic in a **rural, underserved area**? Perhaps that's the direction you'd like your career to take, and, if so, you'll want to seek out medical schools that place a high priority on that area.

- Were the part-time jobs you had with a research firm particularly gratifying? If you'd like to pursue a **research career**, look for schools that have a strong reputation in that area or are known for graduating a large percentage of medical students going into research careers.

- There are also other ways that speak to your interests and career goals. Did you spend your junior year tutoring freshmen and sophomores in entry-level biology or chemistry? Perhaps you'd like to join a **medical school faculty** and educate the next generation of physicians. If so, look for a medical school with a relatively large percentage of their graduates in teaching positions.

Once again, keep in mind that this is a two-way street. While you're looking for a match, so are the schools. Your experiences will provide good insights for the admissions officers and help them determine if your interests and their missions are congruent.

Kicking Off Your Research

There are a number of ways in which you can research schools to identify the ones that best match your own strengths, interests, and goals.

- MSAR Online: Start with the medical school profiles on the web site (*www.aamc.org/msar*). Here, each institution includes a clear mission statement and a description of its selection factors.

- Web Sites and Literature: You'll also want to review information provided by schools themselves. Although the specific content varies by school, each includes detailed material for prospective students.

- Advisors: Your pre-health advisor or career counselor can provide you with insights and often will be able to recommend specific schools likely to be a good "fit." Make sure you don't overlook this resource.

The Educational Program

As you weigh your decision, you'll also want to consider the differences among the educational programs themselves.

- There's very likely going to be a relationship between a school's mission and its **curriculum**. You'll therefore be able to further gauge whether a particular institution's objectives and your interests align by analyzing course requirements and electives programs. A medical school with a mission to graduate more primary care doctors may, for example, have a track that provides for additional training in that area. A school that emphasizes research might have their students devote an extended period of time to scholarly pursuits.

- As you do your research, also consider what **teaching methods** you find most effective. Do you tend to do well with self-directed or participatory learning exercises, or do you do better with the more traditional, lecture-based style of learning? While most medical schools use an educational model that combines various methods, there will be a difference as to precisely how this mix has been adapted. You'll want to explore the degree to which you're likely to find small group discussions and problem-based learning exercises (as examples) versus a traditional teaching approach. A good starting point for your exploration is a school's web site, as well as the AAMC's curriculum directory.

- There are key differences as to **grading intervals** (or systems). Some institutions use a pass/fail system; others an honors/pass/fail system; and still others use letter grades. Some students have definite preferences, and if you're one of them, you may wish to consider a school's grading system as you narrow your selection.

There are many other factors connected with the educational program that you might want to think about. How will you be evaluated? At what point must students pass the first two steps of the United States Medical Licensing Examination (USMLE) before advancing in their education? What level of academic support is available? Is there a mentor system, for instance? What about support services or organizations for cultural and other minorities— are they available? Questions such as these will undoubtedly enter into your final decision as you deliberate between offers, and you may wish to consider them now.

"How Do My Grades and MCAT® Scores Factor In?"

Don't choose schools based solely on where you think your grades and MCAT® scores will be accepted. While there's no question that your educational record is important and that admissions officers seek candidates who are likely to succeed academically in their programs, it's important to realize that **academics alone do not predict who will become an effective physician, and admissions officers know that all too well.**

The very fact that there are so many instances in which a "high scoring" applicant does not receive an acceptance to medical school—and in which an applicant with lower-than- average grades and scores does—tells you that admissions officers must be looking at other factors.

Admissions officers are taking a more "holistic" approach to evaluating their applicants. Through this practice, admissions officers assess their candidates more broadly, looking not only at their "metrics" (GPA and MCAT® scores) but at their experiences and personal attributes, as well.

You can read about the holistic approach to admissions in Chapter 7, "The Admissions Decision."

Attending Medical School in Your "Home" State

State residents enrolled in state-supported medical schools pay lower tuition than nonresidents. In addition to that, though, in-state residents are often given preference for admission (compared to out-of-state residents) for at least some of their places because the school receives state government support. You therefore may want to give strong consideration to the public institution in your state as you decide where to apply.

And many students do just that. Nationally, 61 percent of 2012 matriculants attended schools in their home states.

Public or Private?

You also may be deliberating between public and private institutions. If you're considering a public medical school in your state of residence, one aspect of this decision, as we just mentioned, is likely to be cost. (If you're from out of state, the cost differential between a public institution and a private school virtually disappears. See chart in Chapter 11.) But don't automatically assume, even if you are interested in a state school near your home, that

International Students

There are only a small number of international students—those who are not U.S. citizens or permitted to reside permanently in this country—at U.S. medical schools. If you hope to be among this group, know that private medical schools are more likely to accept international students than public schools, and that most medical schools require completion of premedical coursework at a U.S. college or university.

State Residency Requirements

Requirements are established by state legislatures and are usually available from school officials or the school's (or state's) web site. We encourage you to clarify your official residency status before applying.

the private route will be more expensive under all circumstances. Some private institutions, for example, may have large endowments that allow them to provide significant scholarship aid to qualifying students and thus lower the "effective" tuition rate, permitting those students to graduate with less educational debt than they would have generated if they had attended a public medical school in their "home" state.

But cost is only one consideration. Another element to be aware of when investigating the differences between private and public institutions is the school's mission—and how it might relate to your own aspirations and interests. Although all medical schools—public or private—have different missions, certain public institutions may have specific goals related to their state, such as increasing the supply of physicians there. (If the school is in your home state and you'd like to remain there after graduation, that will be a factor from both your perspective and the school's.) Other public institutions were founded by state legislators with an emphasis on the needs of a particular patient population—such as elder, rural, or underserved groups—which should enter into your evaluation if that objective corresponds to your own.

Additional Factors to Consider

There are many other factors that may be important to you as you search for a good "match." Some of these include:

- **Location**

  Besides the impact of state residency on the costs of a public medical school, there are other aspects to the issue of location and how it factors into your decision where to apply. Perhaps you simply prefer a specific geographic region. Do you, for example, want to be close to family and friends? Do you prefer a warmer (or cooler) climate? Are you a fan of the East coast…or the South…or the West? These factors play to your comfort level, and are all valid considerations. Beyond that, though, location can also relate to your career goals, as well as to a school's mission. If you hope to specialize in geriatrics, for example, a medical school located in an area with a higher-than-average proportion of older adults may be able to provide you with the experience you seek.

  That's looking at it from your perspective. Consider, for a moment, the school's perspective. In some cases, a school may be seeking students from particular geographic regions in order to bolster its diversity, and you'll want to consider the impact—if any—that your own state residence might have on your application to medical schools in other areas.

- **Size and Demographics**

  The size and demographics of the medical school—both in terms of its student body as well as its faculty—may be a consideration for you, as well. The school entries in MSAR Online include data on the prior year's entering class, including the number of students by gender as well as by (self-reported) race and ethnicity.

- **Costs**

  Medical education doesn't come cheap, and the expenses associated with particular institutions will no doubt be a factor in your decision. At this stage, though, you won't know what your actual costs will be (or the degree of assistance you will get) until a school sends you a financial aid package in conjunction with its offer. Still, in looking through the school entries, you can get a general idea as to the relative expenses of various institutions, and you will probably keep that in mind as you narrow your selection.

The Importance of Additional Factors

Just because we call them "additional" doesn't lessen their importance. Below is the percentage to which matriculating students felt specific factors were either a positive or very positive factor in choosing the medical school they now attend:

Factors	Percent
Geographic location of school	81.4
Faculty mentorship	71.4
Diversity of the student body	58.3
Financial costs of attending	54.1
Diversity of the faculty	49.4

Source: AAMC's 2012 Matriculating Student Questionnaire (MSQ)

Special Regional Opportunities

Finally, you should be aware that some states without a public medical school participate in special interstate and regional agreements to provide their residents with access to a medical education. Currently, there are five interstate agreements, listed below:

- The Delaware Institute of Medical Information and Research
  http://dhss.delaware.gov/dhss/dhcc/dimer.html, 1-302-577-3240, 1-800-292-7935

- The Finance Authority of Maine's Access to Medical Education Program
  www.famemaine.com/files/Pages/education/students_and_families/Medical_Education.aspx
  1-800-228-3734

- University of Utah School of Medicine Idaho Contract
  http://medicine.utah.edu/admissions/begin/residency.php, 1-208-282-2475,
  residency@sa.utah.edu

- The Western Interstate Commission for Higher Education
  www.wiche.edu/psep/medi, 1-303-541-0200

- The WWAMI (Washington, Wyoming, Alaska, Montana, and Idaho) Program
  http://uwmedicine.washington.edu/Education/WWAMI/Pages/Medical-School.aspx

You can learn more about each of these regional opportunities by visiting their web sites or calling their program offices.

CHAPTER 6:
Applying to Medical School

Now that you've identified the schools that seem right for you, you're ready to tackle the steps in applying. In this chapter, we'll review the AAMC's American Medical College Application Service (AMCAS®), provide an overview of the application and admissions cycle, talk about your personal statement and letters of evaluation, and give you information about application costs and other specifics.

The Responsibilities of the Medical School Applicant

It is vital that you are aware of the responsibilities you have as an applicant to medical school. These are reviewed at length at the end of this chapter, but here are a few of the most critical:

- Meet all deadlines

- Complete the AMCAS® application accurately

- Know the admission requirements at each school

- Promptly notify AMCAS of any change in contact information

- Respond promptly to interview invitations

- File for financial aid as soon as possible

- Withdraw from the schools you will not attend

Please see "AAMC Recommendations for Medical School and M.D.-Ph.D. Candidates" later in this chapter for details.

American Medical College Application Service (AMCAS®)

Scan this QR code with your smartphone to visit the AMCAS web site, connect with AMCAS on Facebook and Twitter, and watch video tutorials.

You may have heard about AMCAS from your pre-health advisor, career counselor, or even your classmates. In a nutshell, AMCAS is a web-based application processing service offered by the AAMC and utilized by almost every medical school in the country. (For schools that do not participate in AMCAS, see the Non-AMCAS Schools box later in this chapter.) This service does not screen applicants; rather it provides admissions officers with an abundance of information they can use to make preliminary assessments.

This service has benefits to applicants, as well. The most obvious one is that AMCAS allows students to apply to as many medical schools as they want with a single application (although many schools require a "secondary application," a topic we will discuss later in this chapter). Beyond that, it provides applicants with a single point of transmission for official transcripts, letters of evaluation, and other supporting documentation.

Even if you're not yet ready to begin the application process, you might want to go to *www.aamc.org/amcas* for a preview. There, you'll find links to key steps involved in starting

If you have previously registered for the MCAT® exam, the Fee Assistance Program, or other AAMC services, you have already selected an AAMC username and password and received an AAMC ID. **Use this same access information to enter the AMCAS® application site.** If you do not already have an AAMC ID Number, you will need to register online to create a username and password before you begin your application. Visit *www.aamc. org/amcas* when you're ready to begin the application process.

an application, including an application timeline, tips, and checklists useful in completing the application, answers to frequently asked questions, and a comprehensive instruction manual.

Sections of the AMCAS Application

The AMCAS application consists of nine sections. It might sound like a lot, but remember… you don't have to complete it all in one sitting. You can save your work and return to your application as many times as you wish until you've finished it. Here's an overview of what to expect:

1. **Identifying Information.** This section asks you to enter your name, birth information, and sex.

2. **Schools Attended.** Here, you'll enter high school and college information. Once this section (and the identifying information section) is completed, you will be able to create a Transcript Request Form.

3. **Biographic Information.** You'll use this section to enter your address details and information about citizenship, legal residence, ethnicity, languages spoken, and other biographic information.

4. **Course Work.** You'll next enter grades and credits for every course that you have enrolled in at any U.S., U.S. territorial, or Canadian postsecondary institution. (It is important that you provide information for all courses.)

5. **Work/Activities.** Here, you'll enter any work and extracurricular activities, awards, honors, or publications that you would like to bring to the attention of the medical school(s). Up to 15 experiences may be listed.

6. **Letters of Evaluation.** You will use this section to provide information about letters of evaluation that will be submitted to schools on your behalf. (We cover this step in a bit more detail later in this chapter.)

7. **Medical Schools.** In this section, you will designate the medical schools to which you want to submit an application. In addition, you will have an opportunity to designate which letters of evaluation you wish to submit to specific schools.

8. **Personal Statement.** Here, you will compose a personal essay. (We discuss this step more thoroughly later in this chapter, as well.)

9. **Standardized Tests.** And finally…your MCAT® scores. In this section, you'll review your MCAT scores and enter any additional test information such as GRE scores. Please note: MCAT scores earned in 2003 or later will automatically be released to AMCAS, and no further action will be required on your part.

Bear in mind that this is just a brief overview of the AMCAS application. We suggest you read the AMCAS Instruction Manual, available online, and explore the various resources on the AMCAS site at *www.aamc.org/amcas*.

Transcript Requests via AMCAS

In addition to completing your AMCAS application, you must request that an official transcript be forwarded to AMCAS by the registrar of every postsecondary school you've attended. Here again, AMCAS facilitates the application process by providing a Transcript Request Form. This includes junior college, community college, trade school, or other professional school—regardless of whether credit was earned—within the United States, Canada, or U.S. territories. (This requirement also applies to any college courses you took in high school.) For regular applicants, all official transcripts must be received no later than two weeks following the deadline date for application materials. Please refer to the AMCAS Instruction Manual and online Help for detailed information about official transcript requirements.

Limited Changes After Submission

You'll want to check your work carefully before you hit "submit." That's because you're limited in what changes you can make to your application following submission. More specifically, you can make changes to your contact information (such as addresses) and add additional schools or letters of evaluation. Other than these few exceptions, your application will be submitted to schools exactly as you have completed it.

Application Processing and Verification

Once AMCAS has received your submitted application and official transcripts from each postsecondary school at which you've been registered, AMCAS verifies the accuracy of your academic record by comparing the information you entered on the application to that contained in your official transcripts. Once processing has been completed, AMCAS makes the application available to all medical schools you designated and distributes MCAT scores. (As mentioned earlier, MCAT scores from 2003 and later are automatically included; those from years prior to 2003 are provided to medical schools only if the applicant has released those scores to AMCAS.)

The Application and Admissions Cycle

Now that you have an idea as to what the AMCAS process involves, you're likely wondering when it all takes place. Generally speaking, the AMCAS application process opens to students in early May of each year, and participating schools begin receiving applicant data in June.

Also generally speaking, the deadlines for receipt of primary applications to medical schools that participate in AMCAS are from mid-October to mid-December. (See Chapter 6 for information on secondary applications.) Speaking in specifics, though, there is no one application timetable, as each school establishes its own deadlines for receipt of required materials. You can find the dates in medical schools' bulletins and web sites and in the school listings on MSAR Online.

Medical schools vary not only in terms of their application deadlines, but also in the timing by which they make their admissions decisions. Most schools use a system of "rolling admissions," selecting students for interviews (and sending out acceptance letters) as the applications are received, rather than waiting until a specific cut-off date before beginning their decision process. In these instances, schools are likely to have offered admission to some students while others have yet to be interviewed—meaning that you run the risk that a medical school you're interested in fills all slots for its entering class before you've even had a turn at bat! (You can find out if a medical school uses a rolling admissions system by checking its web site.) That's why, when it comes to applying to medical school...the sooner, the better.

As far as interviews go, admissions committees usually meet with candidates from fall through spring, with most interviews held during the winter months. (We discuss this part of the admissions cycle in Chapter 7.) By March 30, medical schools will—by collective agreement—issue a number of acceptances at least equal to the size of their first-year entering class.

Early Decision Programs

One of your first decisions will be whether to apply to a medical school through the Early Decision Program (EDP) or the regular application process. Although criteria for accepting EDP applicants vary among schools, the program frequently requires that applicants show extraordinary credentials.

A small percentage of applicants apply through the EDP, and only about half of medical schools even offer it. You can learn more about program requirements at *www.aamc.org/students/applying/requirements/edp*.

For M.D.-Ph.D. Applicants

Those of you who are applying to M.D.-Ph.D. programs will be required to write two additional essays: a relatively brief one focusing on your reasons for pursuing the combined degree, and a more lengthy one (of about three pages) describing your research activities. You can read more about these additional essays in the AMCAS® Instruction Manual or get further guidance from your pre-health advisor or career counselor.

Personal Statements and Letters of Evaluation

As you'll learn in Chapter 7, admissions officers want to know more about you than just where you went to college, what courses you took and what grades you earned, and how you scored on the MCAT exam. They want to know you at a more personal level. That's why an essay and letters of evaluation are integral components of your application to medical school and part of the AMCAS process.

Your Personal Statement

Every applicant is required to submit a Personal Comments essay of up to 5,300 characters (or approximately one page) in length. This is your opportunity to distinguish yourself from other applicants and provide admissions officers with insights as to why you are interested in medicine—and why you would be a dedicated and effective physician.

You should know that many admissions committees place significant weight on this section, so you should take the time and effort to craft an organized, well-written, and compelling statement. Some questions you may want to consider while formulating your essay are:

- Why have you selected the field of medicine?

- What motivates you to learn more about medicine?

- What do you want medical schools to know about you that hasn't been disclosed in other sections of the application?

In addition, you may wish to include information such as:

- Special hardships, challenges, or obstacles that may have influenced your educational pursuits.

- Commentary on significant fluctuations in your academic record that are not explained elsewhere in your application.

As you begin to carve out your essay, keep in mind that in order to be unique, you must be specific. Rather than write, for example, that *"challenges in my childhood led me to consider medicine at an early age,"* write that *"the summer I turned eight, my 11-year-old sister was diagnosed with Diabetes Type I, and I witnessed first-hand the compassion and understanding with which the doctor dealt with my parents. It was during those first few difficult months that I decided I wanted to be a physician."*

In addition to being specific, you will want to ensure that your essay is persuasive (and interesting), follows a logical and orderly flow, and relates to your reasons for choosing medicine and/or why you believe you will be successful in medical school and as a physician. Beyond that, of course, your writing must adhere to correct grammar and be free of typographical errors and misspellings.

Letters of Evaluation

The Letters of Evaluation section of the AMCAS application enables you to provide information about your letters of evaluation. You can add up to 10 letter entries, but that does not mean medical schools wish to receive 10 letters for each applicant—most schools request only two or three letters. AMCAS allows additional letters so that you have the option to designate specific letters for specific schools.

Medical schools have various requirements regarding letters of evaluation, but they all require them in one form or another. If your college has a pre-health advisor, for example, medical schools will probably require a letter from him or her (or from the pre-health committee, if your school has one) as well as a letter from at least one faculty member. In instances where there is no pre-health advisor, many medical schools may ask for additional letters from faculty— often specifying that at least one comes from a science professor. Still, other medical schools do not specify from where the letters come, welcome additional letters beyond those that are required, and/or limit the number they will accept. In all cases, you should review the web sites of the medical schools for information on their specific letter requirements.

In general, though—and as you would expect—medical schools want letters from those who are in a position to judge your ability to be successful in medical school, which includes not only your academic capabilities and accomplishments, but also your personal characteristics and skills.

Letters provide medical school admission committees with more insight into your abilities, dedication, and unique traits that are evidenced beyond grades, MCAT® scores, and other information that you have provided in your application. You should seek someone who knows you well and whose opinion is likely to be highly valued. (Admissions committees, for example, are not likely to place as much value on the input of your teaching assistant, but they will weigh heavily the thoughts of the chair of the biology department who taught your honors biology class.) In short, letters can be very valuable, and you should be thoughtful in selecting who you will ask to write on your behalf.

Secondary Applications

Your "primary" application is your AMCAS application. In addition, though, about half of all medical schools require school-specific, or "secondary," applications. That's because, while the primary application provides admissions officers with much of the information they need, by its very nature a universal application—such as AMCAS—cannot be "all things to all people" and address issues specific to individual schools. Many institutions therefore require a secondary application that will be used to assess students' reasons for applying to that particular school. (Medical schools will notify you if such an application is needed.) Secondary applications may call for additional letters of evaluation, supplementary writing samples, and/or updated transcripts. Go to the web sites of the medical schools in which you are interested to learn more.

Costs of Applying

The fees associated with applying to medical school fall into four general categories:

Primary Application
For the 2013 entering class, the fee was $160 for the first school and $34 for each additional school. (Remember, too, that there are several schools that do not use AMCAS and that you may incur a different fee in those instances.)

Secondary Application
Fees for secondary applications typically range from $25 to $100.

College Service Fees
There is usually a small fee for transmittal of your transcript from your college registrar and occasionally a fee for transmittal of letters of evaluation.

MCAT® Exam Fees
Although technically not an "application" fee, the costs associated with the MCAT exam are a necessary component of the overall process. Registration for the MCAT exam is $270 and covers the cost of the exam as well as distribution of your scores. In addition, you may incur fees for late registration, changes to your registration, or testing at international test sites. You can read more about the MCAT exam in Chapter 4 and at the MCAT web site (*www.aamc.org/mcat*).

Go to *www.aamc.org/firstfacts* for more information on the costs of applying.

Criminal Background Check

The AAMC has initiated a national background check service through which Certiphi Screening, Inc. (a Vertical Screen® Company) will obtain a background report on all accepted applicants to participating medical schools. This service benefits both medical schools and applicants alike, filling the needs of schools to obtain criminal background checks, while, at the same time, preventing applicants from paying additional fees to each medical school to which they are accepted. For more information, please go to *www.aamc.org/amcascbc*.

You should be aware that participating medical schools may continue to require applicants to undergo a separate national background check process, if required to do so by their own institutional regulations or by applicable state law.

Fee Assistance Program (FAP)

The AAMC believes that the cost of applying to medical school should not be a financial barrier to those interested in becoming physicians.

The AAMC Fee Assistance Program (FAP) assists MCAT® examinees and AMCAS® applicants who, without financial assistance, would be unable to take the MCAT exam or apply to medical schools that use the AMCAS application.

FAP Award Benefits

As of January 3, 2013, applicants who are approved for fee assistance in the current calendar year will receive the following:

MCAT® Benefits

- Reduced Registration Fee for 2013 MCAT exam dates ($100 instead of $270).

- After MCAT registration, FAP awardees also receive support to help prepare for the MCAT exam:

  - a free copy of the book, *The Official Guide to the MCAT® Exam* ($30 value)

  - an authorization code for access to "The Official MCAT® Self-Assessment Package" ($104 value)

  - Financial Assistance for the MCAT exam is available for Psychoeducational or Medical Re-Evaluations as well. The AAMC is pleased to offer this assistance to qualified individuals who need updated psycho-educational or medical evaluations to complete their applications for MCAT® accommodations. For more information, visit *www.aamc.org/students/applying/mcat/accommodations/financial/*.

Note: The MCAT preparation benefits will only be received once, regardless of the number of times the FAP benefit is awarded.

*Fee Assistance Program eligibility decisions are tied directly to the U.S. Department of Health and Human Services' poverty-level guidelines. For the 2013 calendar year, applicants whose total family income is 300 percent or less of the poverty level for their family size are eligible for fee assistance.

MSAR® Benefits

Complimentary access to the MSAR Online and the *MSAR: Getting Started* guidebook (e-book) for one year from the date of activation ($30 value).

AMCAS® Benefits

Waiver for all AMCAS fees for up to 14 medical schools ($602 value).
However, additional fees will be charged for each designation beyond the initial set of 14.

For more information, see *www.aamc.org/students/applying/fap/benefits/*

Special Note About Deferred Entry

In recent years, most medical schools have developed delayed matriculation policies to allow their accepted applicants to defer entry without giving up their medical school places. Deferrals are only granted after acceptance. These programs usually require that the applicant submit a written request, and some schools may also ask for a report at the end of the deferral period. Delays of matriculation are usually granted for one year, although some schools may occasionally defer for longer periods of time. Some institutions may require delayed matriculants to sign an agreement to not apply to other medical schools in the interim, while others permit application to other schools. Interested applicants should seek specific information from schools where they applied.

AAMC Recommendations for Medical School and M.D.-Ph.D. Candidates

To help ensure that all M.D. and M.D.-Ph.D. candidates are provided timely notification of the outcome of their application and timely access to available first-year positions, and that schools and programs are protected from having unfilled positions in their entering classes, the Association of American Medical Colleges has distributed the following recommendations. They are provided for the information of prospective students, their advisors, and personnel at the medical schools and programs to which they apply. The AAMC recommends that:

1. Each applicant be familiar with, understand, and comply with the application, acceptance, and admission procedures at each school or program to which the applicant has applied, as well as with these Recommendations.

2. Each applicant provide accurate and truthful information in all aspects of the application, acceptance, and admission processes for each school or program to which the applicant has applied.

3. Each applicant submit all application documents (e.g., primary and secondary application forms, transcript[s], letters of evaluation, fees) to each school in a timely manner and no later than the school's or program's published deadline date.

4. Each applicant promptly notify all relevant medical school application services and all medical schools or programs with independent application processes of any change, permanent or temporary, in contact information (e.g., mailing address, telephone number, e-mail address).

5. Any applicant who will be unavailable for an extended period of time (e.g., foreign travel, vacation, holidays) during the application/admission process:

    a. Provide instructions regarding his or her application and the authority to respond to offers of acceptance to a parent or other responsible individual in the applicant's absence.

    b. Inform all schools or programs at which the applicant remains under consideration of this individual's name and contact information.

6. Each applicant respond promptly to a school's or program's invitation for interview. Any applicant who cannot appear for a previously scheduled interview should notify the school or program immediately of the cancellation of the appointment in the manner requested by the school or program.

7. Each applicant in need of financial aid initiate, as early as possible, the steps necessary to determine eligibility, including the early filing of appropriate need analysis forms and the encouragement of parents, when necessary, to file required income tax forms.

8. In fairness to other applicants, when an applicant has made a decision, prior to May 15, April 30 for M.D.-Ph.D. applicants, not to attend a medical school or program that has made an offer of acceptance, the applicant promptly withdraw his or her application from that (those) other school(s) or program(s) by written correspondence delivered by regular or electronic methods.

9. By May 15 of the matriculation year (April 15 for schools whose first day of class is on or before July 30), April 30 for M.D.-Ph.D. programs, each applicant who has received an offer of acceptance from more than one school or program choose the specific school or program at which the applicant prefers to enroll and withdraw his or her application, by written correspondence delivered by regular or electronic methods, from all other schools or programs from which acceptance offers have been received.

10. Immediately upon enrollment in, or initiation of an orientation program immediately prior to enrollment at, a U.S. or Canadian school or program, each applicant withdraw his or her application from consideration at all other schools or programs at which he or she remains under consideration.

Approved: Council of Deans Administrative Board, February 17, 2009

CHAPTER 7:
The Admissions Decision

So much seems to come down to this moment. The years of college study and extracurricular activities, the MCAT® exam and application process, the campus tours and interviews—all culminate as you learn whether the admissions committee at the medical school(s) of your choice has offered you a slot in its entering class.

You know how you chose to which schools to apply. How do schools choose which applicants to accept?

AAMC Recommends a Holistic Approach...

In its *Handbook for Admissions Officers*, the AAMC clearly states that admissions committees have a responsibility to "create a process that identifies applicants whose life experiences, personal attributes, level of academic achievement and career goals conform to those of the institution and who are most likely to contribute to, and benefit from, the school's learning climate."

Source: AAMC Handbook for Admissions Officers

AAMC Podcast on Holistic Admissions

Go to *www.aamc.org/podcasts* for this and other AAMC podcasts. You can subscribe at no charge at the iTunes store.

The Holistic Review of Medical School Applicants

Holistic. What does that mean, and how does it enter into the admissions review process?

Holistic review is defined as a flexible, individualized way of assessing an applicant's capabilities by which balanced consideration is given to experiences, attributes, and academic metrics (E-A-M) and, when considered in combination, how the individual might contribute value as a medical student and future physician. Admissions committees intentionally select individual applicants with the purpose of composing a broadly diverse medical school class in pursuit of achieving a mission.

Each medical school's admissions office has an evaluation process directly linked to the mission, goals, and diversity interests of the institution. They decide which applicants will best serve the needs of its patients, community and the medical profession at large, contribute to the diversity that will drive excellence in the school's learning environment, and benefit most from the school's educational program. Schools look for applicants who have developed a track record that demonstrates the knowledge, skills, attitudes, and behaviors that will best prepare them to fulfill particular challenges. Depending upon its mission, one school might look for applicants who demonstrate service to communities underserved by the current healthcare system, while another may seek applicants who have shown creativity and independent productivity in scholarly activities.

Admissions officers carefully review a multitude of criteria—rather than emphasize just one or two facets—in order to gain an appreciation of the "whole" person. Take, for example, the erroneous belief among many applicants that admissions officers weigh high GPAs and MCAT® scores above all else. While these academic metrics are important components of the admissions decision, they are only one part of the overall package. These scores may need to be considered in context of other responsibilities and what that may communicate about an applicant's ability to balance multiple priorities, maintain a sense of responsibility or resilience. That explains why there are so many instances in which a high-scoring student with a near-perfect GPA does not get into medical school, and why many of those with scores and grades below the average do.

Obviously, something more than academic metrics enters into the admissions decision.

In fact, according to a survey of medical schools conducted by the AAMC, the #1 factor that determines your acceptance to medical school is...the interview. It all ties back to the fact that schools have different missions, and that it is during the interview that admissions officers can really get a sense of who you are and how well your interests and aspirations align with their own goals and purpose. If that sounds familiar, it should. It's the flip side to the analysis you did while you were searching for the "right" schools, analyzing the goals and philosophies of individual schools to determine where you would best fit. Now, it's the medical school's turn to do the same thing from its perspective.

Experiences

Your experiences convey a lot about your interests, your responsibilities, your capabilities, and your knowledge. As a result, medical schools take a close look at what you've learned from where you've been up to this stage in your life. It helps them gauge not only how likely you are to be successful in their programs, but to what degree you will support their mission and contribute as a physician.

We mentioned in the chapter on undergraduate preparation how important your extracurricular activities may be to an admissions committee, and we don't mean just those clubs and organizations within your college. We mean outside of school, as well. Your experience—particularly that related to medical or clinical work—is an important component of your appeal as a candidate to medical school. If you are balancing a 20-30 hour/week job to pay for school while attending classes, that experience is important for admissions committees to know about. It communicates information about your different attributes and also provides additional context for interpreting grades.

Beyond that, the degree to which you contributed in these activities is vital, too. Medicals schools value a demonstration of true commitment, so if you have made a significant contribution or impact on an organization, you'll want to make that clear to the admissions committee. What you learned from your participation in a particular situation is equally of value to admissions committees, who are interested not only in what you've done, but how you think those experiences have influenced who you are and what you want to do.

Here again, the mission of each school will play a large part in how it evaluates your experiences. Institutions with a stated goal of increasing the number of physicians practicing in underserved areas will look with great interest on the summer you spent volunteering in a clinic in a rural location or urban area. In general, though, medical schools especially value community or volunteer experience related to the healthcare field.

Concept of "Distance Traveled"

There's another element we'd like to draw to your attention. Admissions officers are likely to place significance on any obstacles or hardships you've overcome to get to this point in your education. This is a concept known as "distance traveled," and medical schools view life challenges you've faced and conquered as admirable experience—and indicative of some very positive traits. As with other experiences, you can help the admissions committee better understand and appreciate your unique contributions by not only describing the experience, but also what you learned from this perspective.

Attributes

Admissions committees want to know if you have what it takes to become a competent and compassionate doctor. You've got to have the ability to master the science and medicine behind it all, of course, but you also must have some key personal attributes.

Are you empathetic? Do you have integrity? Can you communicate effectively? Traits such as these are necessary to develop into the kind of physician we need for the future, and admissions committees will use a number of means to determine if you possess them. While your experiences can help demonstrate your proficiency in these areas (volunteering for three consecutive summers at a medical clinic certainly conveys dedication, for instance), admissions committees will look to your personal statement, letters of evaluation, and interview(s) to gauge whether you have the desire to build upon these characteristics in medical school.

Medical schools analyze a broad range of attributes, including those related to the applicant's skills and abilities, personal and professional characteristics, and demographic factors. Examples follow.

- **Skills and abilities** could include active listening, critical thinking, and multilingual ability

- **Personal and professional characteristics** could include resilience, intellectual curiosity, and empathy

- **Demographic factors** could include socioeconomic status, race, and gender

We've listed many of the attributes that admissions committees consider in evaluating their application. In addition to these general qualities, though, remember that medical schools give weight to specific characteristics in alignment with their missions. Examples could include research inquisitiveness, empathy, teamwork, curiosity, and a desire for knowledge about health care delivery systems.

Academic metrics

Admissions committees need to determine if you have the academic skills and knowledge necessary to successfully complete the medical school program. To a large extent, committee members will look to your academic record and MCAT® scores to answer those questions. Taken together, these two measures may interact with and inform each other to provide objective information about your knowledge and ability.

Academic History

Your academic history helps admission committees establish whether your study skills, persistence, course of study, and grades predict success in their medical school. Committee members are able to make this determination, to a significant degree, by reviewing your college transcript. More specifically, committee members consider:

- Grades earned in each course and laboratory

- Grade trends in the last two years of schooling

- Number of credit hours carried in each academic period

- Distribution of coursework among the biological, physical, and social sciences and the humanities

- Need for remediation of unsatisfactory academic work

- Number of incomplete grades and course withdrawals

- Number of years taken to complete the degree program

MCAT® Scores

The ability of admission committees to predict success is heightened when they add MCAT® scores into the mix. That's because, as you probably already know, there can be significant differences in grading scales and standards from college to college, and MCAT® scores

Although each medical school establishes its own criteria, schools usually prefer applicants who balanced science and humanities coursework, carried respectable course loads, and, generally speaking, earned 3.0–4.0 grades (on a 4.0 scale).

See Chapter 10 for information on the range of GPA averages of all applicants for the 2012 entering class. Or, for the range of GPAs of accepted applicants to a particular medical school, see that institution's entry in MSAR Online.

You can gain some insights by reviewing the charts in chapter 10, which shows what percentage of applicants were accepted to medical school based on combinations of specific grades and scores. In addition, in the MSAR Online include the range of MCAT® scores generally deemed acceptable for admission, along with the median overall GPA and science GPA of their accepted students.

provide admissions officers with a standardized measure by which to compare applicants. In fact, the ability of admissions officers to predict who will be successful in the first two years of their programs increases by as much as 50 percent (gauging by first- and second-year medical school grades) when they look at MCAT® scores in conjunction with undergraduate GPAs as opposed to grades alone.

As a result, the better your grades and higher your scores, the more likely you are to be accepted. It is important to remember, though, that there is still a wide range of MCAT® scores and GPAs found among accepted applicants, and that scores and grades are used in conjunction with other factors as discussed earlier in this chapter.

Making the Evaluation

Admission committees gauge all three of these areas—experience, attributes, and academic metrics—and how they relate to each other in several ways.

First, areas connected with the application process speak to your experience and attributes. Your personal statement, as mentioned in Chapter 6, provides the opportunity for you to tell committee members of your extracurricular activities, "distance traveled" (if applicable; see earlier in this chapter), volunteer efforts, and medical-related work experience—and, by inference, the personal attributes that go along with that. A role as the officer in a school club conveys leadership experience. Working in a medical clinic summer after summer demonstrates motivation for medicine. A long history of volunteering with fundraisers for cancer research certainly suggests teamwork and compassion.

Your letters of evaluation, also described in Chapter 6, attest to your personal attributes, as well. You'll certainly want your professors and advisor (and other evaluators) to address your persistence, strong work habits, and self-discipline. (The faculty and administrative staff at your undergraduate school will know how to craft a letter, but for others, you might want to suggest a few key concepts.)

Then there are the academic metrics. As you know, your academic record is part of your AMCAS® application and includes both your college transcript(s) and MCAT® scores. From there, committee members can determine whether you have the grades, range of coursework, and foundation of knowledge they seek in their successful applicants.

The Interview Is Key

If you've been invited to an interview, you've already impressed your reviewers with your strong personal statement, background, letters of evaluation, and academic history. Now, you have an opportunity to "shine." Medical schools usually interview three, four, even five times as many applicants as their class size, and that is why the interview is likely to be the #1 determining factor at this phase in the assessment as to whether or not you receive an acceptance.

The very fact that interviews are given at all, by the way, is a significant distinction of medical schools, since some professional schools do not necessarily require them. This alone attests to the degree to which admissions officers seek—and medical schools value—qualities and characteristics such as empathy, self-awareness, communications ability, and interpersonal skills that can best be judged in a direct interview situation. You can take a number of steps to ensure you're prepared for it:

- *Know the Basics*

  Whether it's for a new job or for a seat in a medical school's entering class, certain similarities exist in all interviewing situations. A good start would be to pick up one of any of the dozens of books on interviewing skills and familiarize yourself with the basics.

When It's Your Turn to Ask the Questions...

There will come a point in your interview when you will be asked if you have any questions, and it's an opportunity you don't want to pass up. Not only can you clarify any remaining issues, but you'll have another means by which you can demonstrate your commitment, astuteness, and interest in that particular school. With that in mind, you'll want to prepare two or three questions specific to that very school.

Need a way to generate ideas? Check out the AAMC's "Thirty-Five Questions I Wish I Had Asked" at *www.aamc.org/students/applying/310556/ selectingamedicalschoolthirty- fivequestionsiwishihadasked.html.*

AAMC Podcast on Interviewing Basics!

What Are the Basics About Interviewing for Medical School?

Sunny Gibson, director of the Office of Minority and Cultural Affairs at the Feinberg School of Medicine at Northwestern University, goes into careful detail on how to prepare for and increase your chances of success in the interview process while applying to medical school.

Go to www.aamc.org/podcasts/ aspiringdocs/ for podcasts provided by the AAMC and Aspiring Docs. You can subscribe at no charge at the iTunes store.

- *Know What Type of Interview to Expect*

  It will also be helpful to be ready for any number of different interview formats. At some schools, interviews are held with individual admission committee members; at others, group interviews are the norm. In addition, while most interviews are typically held on the medical school campus, some schools have designated interviewers in different geographic regions to minimize time and expense for applicants. (Information about a school's interview policies and procedures is usually provided to applicants in the initial stages of the selection process.)

- *Be Comfortable with Different Interviewing Styles*

  You've probably had some experience interviewing for summer and part-time jobs (and possibly for your undergraduate school), so it won't surprise you that interviewers have their own styles and follow different formats. Some follow a structured design, asking questions from a predetermined list and assigning numeric scores to each answer. Others prefer a more free-flowing arrangement and provide the applicant with a greater degree of open input. Still others fall somewhat in the middle. Again, be ready for any approach.

- *Do Your Research*

  Investigate the school thoroughly by reviewing its profile on the MSAR Online, its web site, the information packet sent to you, and any articles you can get your hands on. Try to talk with current students to get an accurate sense of what the school is like from a student perspective. You'll want to impress your interviewer with not only your potential for success but also your interest in his or her specific institution. You can demonstrate these qualities through the answers to the interviewer's questions as well as by the questions you ask.

- *Practice*

  Since most admission committee members are experienced interviewers who want to learn about the "real" person, you should be forthright and open in your meeting and not try to "game" the interviewer. If you're apprehensive about the process, find a trusted advisor or friend with whom you can conduct mock interviews to help build your confidence.

  Remember, the interview provides applicants with opportunities to discuss their personal histories and motivation for a medical career and to draw attention to any aspects of their application that merit emphasis or explanation. Make certain you present yourself in the best possible light by preparing thoroughly for your meeting. Think about how you conduct yourself among current students and staff during informal meetings, too. These interactions still create an impression of who you are and how you present yourself may come up during a post-interview discussion.

Although interviewers are instructed by admissions officers and guided by federal statutes on what are unfair or discriminatory pre-admission inquiries, there may be an occasion when an interviewer asks an inappropriate question. (See examples in box at right.)

You have the right not to answer what you sense is an inappropriate question. If such a question is asked, try to relax and provide a thoughtful and articulate response (two essential characteristics of a good physician). You may also respectfully decline to answer the question and explain that you were advised not to answer questions that you sensed were inappropriate.

You have the responsibility to report being asked an inappropriate question to help prevent further occurrences. Medical schools have the responsibility to establish procedures that enable applicants to report such incidents in a confidential manner. Medical schools should inform applicants of these procedures prior to interviews and assure them that reporting an incident will not bias the applicant's evaluation.

If a medical school did not inform you of its procedure and an incident occurs, use these guidelines. If possible, report in confidence the interviewer's name and the interview question(s) that was asked to an admissions officer during the interview day. Otherwise, e-mail this informaton to an admisisons officer within 24 hours of the interview noting the date and time of the incident. Furthermore, you have the right to ask if another interview is deemed necessary to ensure an unbiased evaluation of your application to that medical school.

Some interviewers use the interview to assess how well you function under stress and may purposely ask challenging questions to observe how you respond under pressure. How you communicate will be a critical part of the encounter; however, this does not give an interviewer the right to ask you inappropriate questions in their attempt to challenge you during the interview.

Examples of inappropriate questions:

- What is your race, ethnicity, religion, sexual orientation, political affiliation, marital status, opinion on abortion and/or euthanasia, income, value of your home, credit score, etc.?
- Are you planning on having children during medical school?
- Do you have any disabilities?
- Will you require special accommodations?
- Have you ever been arrested?
- Have you ever done drugs?
- How old are you?

Sample response to an inappropriate questions:

Q. *What are your plans for expanding your family during medical school?*

A. Can you please clarify your question? I want to make sure that I'm providing information that is most relevant to my candidacy.

Q. *Have you ever done drugs?*

A. I am uncomfortable discussing my medical history and possible use of prescription medications during this interview.

CHAPTER 8:
Building Toward Greater Diversity

The very process of education itself is enhanced when the student body includes individuals from varying cultures and backgrounds—and research supports this statement. Over the past 40 years, many studies on undergraduate campuses have attested to the value of diversity in the classroom and the overall school environment. It generates a wealth of ideas, helps students challenge their assumptions, and broadens their perspectives. Diversity in group settings has even been linked to greater cognitive results, ultimately leading to better learning outcomes.*

It is for these reasons that the AAMC strives to increase diversity among medical school applicants and therefore offers students a wide range of programs and resources to help meet that goal. Similarly, medical schools themselves have programs—and staff—to ensure that all candidates to their institutions have an equal opportunity for admittance.

Benefits of Diversity Extend Beyond Education*

Increased diversity brings with it benefits that extend beyond the classroom. For example, a greater degree of diversity:

- **Increases access to health care**
  Research has shown that diversity in the physician workforce contributes to increased access to health care.

- **Accelerates advances in research**
  Diversity among clinician-scientists has been linked to an increase in research dedicated to diseases that disproportionately affect racial and ethnic minorities.

Defining Diversity

First…what exactly do we mean by "diversity"?

When you mention the word, diversity, many people automatically think in terms of race and ethnicity. And while it is certainly true that it is important to attract more racial and ethnic minority populations to medicine, the concept of diversity is much more expansive. Diversity refers to the richness of human differences—socioeconomic status, race, ethnicity, language, nationality, sex, gender identity, sexual orientation, religion, geography, disability, age, and individual aspects such as personality, learning styles, and life experiences. Let's look at diversity based on available AAMC data and other information.

- **First, consider race and ethnicity.** While diversity extends beyond this particular characteristic it remains a critical component. The data show, for example, that only 6.1 percent of matriculating students are black or African American, 9.2 percent are Hispanic or Latino, and .3 percent are American Indian or Alaska Native.

- **What about family income?** This is another area of great imbalance. Parental income of students entering medical school skews heavily to the upper range, with median income of $115,000. (That's almost double the estimated U.S. median family income of $62,000 reported by the U.S. Census Bureau.) Looking at it from another angle, almost one in six students come from homes in which their parents earn $250,000 or more a year.

*See list of suggested readings and resources at the end of this chapter to learn more about diversity in educational settings.

Low-Income Households Are Underrepresented...

Parental Income of Entering Medical Students, 2012

Income	Percent
Less than $10,000	2.7
$10,000 - $19,999	2.3
$20,000 - $29,999	3.7
$30,000 - $39,999	3.9
$40,000 - $49,999	3.9
$50,000 - $74,999	12.3
$75,000 - $99,999	10.5
$100,000 - $249,999	42.7
$250,000 - $499,999	14.6
$500,000 or more	3.3
Median income of parents	$115,000

Source: AAMC's 2012 Matriculating Student Questionnaire (MSQ)

...As Are Racial Ethnic Minorities

Demographics of Entering Medical Students*, 2012

Demographic	Percent
American Indian or Alaska Native	0.3
Hispanic/Latino	8.9
Black or African American	6.1
Asian	20.8
White	56.4

*self-identified. Source: AAMC Data Warehouse, 2012

- **Another perspective—gender**. On the surface, it appears that male and female applicants are fairly equal in number, but there are instances where that is not the case. You'll see, for example, from the chart below left, that there is a relative shortage of male applicants within the black or African American demographic. Within this specific group, males comprise barely one-third of those who apply to medical school.

Chart 8-A

Applicants* to U.S. Medical Schools by Race, Ethnicity, and Sex, 2012

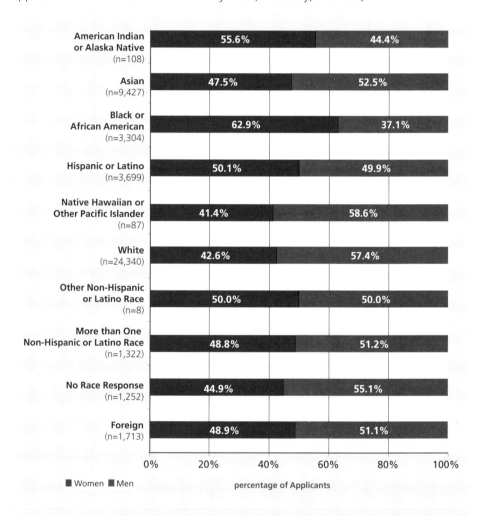

Note: 6 applicants who declined to report gender were not included in this figure.
*Includes Cuban, Mexican American, Puerto Rican, Other Hispanic, Multiple Hispanic.
Source: https://www.aamc.org/data/facts/applicantmatriculant/. (Table 12)

AAMC Programs and Resources

With the benefits that diversity offers, the AAMC is strongly committed to improving health for all. To that end, the AAMC is engaged in a number of programs and initiatives to help increase diversity and open the campus gates to capable and promising students from a broad range of backgrounds. (It's important to note that while these programs are open to all, they are sensitive to the challenges and needs of individuals from groups underrepresented in medicine.) These initiatives are described below.

Career Fairs and Enrichment Programs

Medical schools throughout the country provide various programs and resources designed to recruit students and prepare them for medical education. Some of these programs are held during the school year, others in the summer. They are designed for high school students, college students, and those who have completed undergraduate study.

The AAMC is affiliated with two such programs:

- ***Minority Student Medical Career Awareness Workshops and Recruitment Fair***
  This event is held each fall in conjunction with the AAMC Annual Meeting. Students are encouraged to come and "Explore the Possibilities in Medicine." College and high school students, parents, prehealth advisors, school administrators, and other interested individuals can meet diversity affairs and admissions officers from U.S. medical schools and other health professions schools to discuss medical school preparation, enrichment programs, admission policies and procedures, financial aid and more. Attendees can also participate in interactive medical and health activities and workshops. For more information, visit *www.aamc.org/medicalcareerfair*.

- ***Summer Medical and Dental Education Program (SMDEP)***
  The Summer Medical and Dental Education Program is a free six-week summer academic enrichment program for college freshmen and sophomores interested in careers in medicine or dentistry. Components of the program include science and mathematics-based courses, learning and study skills seminars, career development activities, clinical experiences, and a financial planning workshop. Funded by the Robert Wood Johnson Foundation and offered at 12 U.S. medical and 9 dental schools across the nation, the program includes a stipend, housing, and meals. For additional information, visit *www.smdep.org*, or call toll-free at 1-866-58SMDEP.

Aspiring Docs is an AAMC program to increase diversity in medicine.

It's vital for tomorrow's medical students to be diverse in race, ethnicity, gender, religion, socio economic status, and sexual orientation, as well as express diversity in experience and thought. Having a diverse workforce of doctors is essential to providing the best care for all communities and improving the health of our nation.

Aspiring Docs offers the most reliable tools and information to anyone considering a career in medicine. Visit *www.aamc.org/aspiringdocs* to access the growing library of information and resources.

Other AAMC Resources

The AAMC also offers a wide variety of publications, online tools, and other information in the "Minorities in Medicine" section of the AAMC's web site at *www.aamc.org/students/ minorities* and the AAMC's Diversity web site at *www.aamc.org/diversity*. Among the resources you will find there are:

- **Medical Students with Disabilities: Resources to Enhance Accessibility**
  This recently published guide book informs users about current resources available to medical schools as they accept and matriculate a growing number of medical students with a wide range of disabilities. Specifically there is an emphasis in this publication on the assistive technologies available for medical students. You can order a copy of this guide book at *https://members.aamc.org/eweb/DynamicPage. aspx?webcode=PubHome*.

- **Enrichment programs online**
  This site includes a free database to help students locate summer enrichment programs on medical school campuses. You can search by school, state, region, area of focus, and length of program. Go to *https://services.aamc.org/summerprograms/* to explore programs of interest.

- **Medical Minority Applicant Registry**
  During the MCAT registration, students applying to medical school who are economically disadvantaged or are from racial and ethnic groups that are historically underrepresented in medicine can select the Med-MAR option to be included in the registry. This web-based program provides medical schools with basic biographical information and MCAT scores of registered examinees, thereby proving institutions with opportunities to enhance their diversity efforts. Go to *www.aamc.org/medmar* for more information.

  For information about the definition of underrepresented in medicine, www.aamc.org/urm.

- **Fee Assistance Program (FAP)**
  The AAMC offers its Fee Assistance Program to students whose financial limitations would otherwise prevent them from taking the MCAT® exam or applying to medical school. Details about the FAP can be found at *www.aamc.org/fap* and in Chapter 6 of this book.

- **Data about Applicants, Matriculants, and Graduates**
  The AAMC also collects and presents detailed data about medical students from an array of racial and ethnic groups, most of which are available online free-of-charge on the AAMC web site (and a good deal of which is included in this guide). Several resources likely to be of interest are:

  — AAMC information about recent matriculant data for each medical school is presented in this chapter in Table 8-A, Matriculants by Medical School and Race and Ethnicity, 2012.

  — Chapter 10 includes a table showing the self-reported racial and ethnic identification of medical school applicants and accepted applicants for the 2012 entering class.

  — A large collection of data about medical school applicants, matriculants, and graduates are available on the AAMC web site at *www.aamc.org/facts*.

  — The AAMC publication, Diversity in Medical Education, Facts & Figures 2012, provides race and ethnicity data on medical school applicants, accepted applicants, matriculants, enrollment, graduates, and faculty. You can access the full text without charge at *www.aamc.org/students/minorities*.

  — Data on medical school faculty, including information by race and ethnicity, can be found at *www.aamc.org/data/facultyroster/reports*.

For those who wish to explore the benefits of diversity, may we suggest the following readings:

Antonio AL, Chang MJ, Hakuta K, Kenny DA, Levin S, Milem JF. *Effects of racial diversity on complex thinking in college students.* Psychological Science. 2004:15;507-10.

Astin AW. *What matters in college? Four critical years revisited.* San Francisco, CA:Jossey-Bass, 1993.

Gurin P. *The compelling need for diversity in higher education: Expert testimony in Gratz, et al. v. Bollinger, et al.* Michigan J of Race & Law. 1999:5; 363–425.

Nemeth CJ, Wachtler J. *Creative problem solving as a result of majority vs. minority influence.* European J of Social Psychology, 1983:13; 45–55.

Saha S; Guiton G; Wimmers PF.; Wilkerson L. *Student Body Racial and Ethnic Composition and Diversity-Related Outcomes in US Medical Schools.* Journal of the American Medical Association, JAMA, 2008. 300: 1135–1145.

Smith DG & Associates. *Diversity works: The emerging picture of how students benefit.* Washington, DC: Association of American Colleges and Universities, 1997.

Smith DG; *Diversity's Promise for Higher Education: Making It Work.* Baltimore, MD; The Johns Hopkins University Press, 2009.

Whitla, D.K., Orfield, G., Silen, W., Teperow, C., Howard, C., & Reede, J. (2003). *Educational Benefits of Diversity in Medical School: A survey of students.* Academic Medicine. 2003; 78: 460-466.

School Programs and Resources

It's not just the AAMC that's committed to the issue of diversity. As you would expect, colleges and medical schools are also committed to making medical education accessible to all individuals—and you'll certainly want to take advantage of these resources as well. Among them are:

- *Pre-medical school programs at undergraduate colleges*

  Pre-health advisors have an abundance of pertinent information at their fingertips. Not only can they help you with the application process and refer you to appropriate contacts, they also know about programs that students from underrepresented groups and disadvantaged backgrounds are likely to find useful. If your college has a pre-health advisor (and the majority of them do), make sure you take advantage of this valuable resource. Learn more about pre-health advisors at *www.naahp.org*.

- *Medical School web sites*

  You'll also want to explore the medical school web sites for information on their diversity programs and resources. Go to *www.aamc.org/medicalschools* for a listing of all U.S. and Canadian M.D.-granting medical schools and links to their web sites.

- *Medical school diversity affairs representatives*

  Another invaluable resource will be the medical school diversity affairs representatives. These individuals are dedicated to increasing diversity among medical schools at their institutions and are an excellent source of information for applicants (or potential applicants). You can get the name of the diversity affairs contacts at any U.S. medical school through the Directory of Diversity Affairs Representatives searchable database. It is search able by name, location, and institution, and is available at *www.aamc.org/coda*.

- *Financial assistance for medical school*

  Don't let the cost of medical school deter you from your dreams. As you'll learn in Chapter 11 of this publication, more than four-fifths of medical students across the country receive some form of financial assistance. Medical schools—both public and private—work hard to offer a variety of financial aid plans to ensure that capable students are not denied access to their institutions as a result of financial limitations. In addition to discussing possibilities for assistance with the financial aid officer at the medical schools that interest you, you should familiarize yourself with general information about financing a medical education by reading the relevant material in this book, reviewing the wealth of information about loans (and other programs) at *www.aamc.org/first*.

- *Programs at medical schools*

  Once you've enrolled in medical school, you'll find that a variety of academic and personal support programs are available to you. These programs assist students from various backgrounds to successfully complete their medical studies, with the ultimate goal of increasing diversity among physicians entering careers in patient care, teaching, and research, and of eliminating racial and ethnic disparities in health care.

No Advisor? Contact the NAAHP for Help

If your institution does not have a pre-health advisor, you can contact the National Association of Advisors for the Health Professions (NAAHP). There, you will find a list of NAAHP members who have volunteered to help students without access to a pre-health advisor. Learn more about what pre-health advisors do and how to locate one at *http://naahp.org/Default.aspx?tabid=3238*.

	School	Mexican American	Cuban	Puerto Rican	Other Hispanic or Latino	Total Hispanic or Latino	Chinese	Asian Indian	Pakistani	Filipino	Japanese	Korean	Vietnamese	Other Asian	Total Asian	Native American (incl AK)	Black	Native Hawaiian /OPI	White	Unduplicated
AL	Alabama	1	0	0	1	2	9	11	1	1	1	2	2	2	29	3	6	0	140	176
	South Alabama	0	0	0	1	1	1	5	1	1	0	0	0	1	8	1	4	1	59	74
AR	Arkansas	3	1	1	2	7	6	6	4	2	0	2	3	3	22	0	7	0	142	166
AZ	Arizona	5	1	0	3	8	10	9	0	3	3	5	2	3	30	1	0	1	81	115
	Arizona Phoenix	2	0	0	0	2	0	6	2	2	1	1	0	3	15	1	1	0	59	80
CA	Loma Linda	5	2	4	10	17	13	4	0	3	4	6	4	6	54	1	11	0	94	168
	Southern Cal-Keck	10	1	1	9	19	35	16	0	4	7	8	1	9	73	1	11	0	93	184
	Stanford	5	0	0	3	8	18	14	3	2	2	7	3	4	45	0	4	1	37	92
	UC Berkeley/SF Joint Prog	2	0	1	1	4	3	2	0	0	0	1	1	1	7	0	0	0	7	16
	UC Davis	13	0	0	4	17	5	5	1	5	3	4	14	1	43	6	5	0	50	109
	UC Irvine	9	0	0	8	16	11	11	1	1	4	5	4	3	37	2	3	0	58	104
	UC San Diego	9	1	1	7	17	25	10	0	2	2	3	2	4	44	2	6	2	72	125
	UC San Francisco	15	1	2	6	22	31	6	3	3	3	5	5	5	53	2	14	1	79	149
	UCLA Drew	6	0	0	1	7	1	0	0	2	1	1	2	1	8	2	10	0	2	24
	UCLA-Geffen	15	0	1	6	21	33	19	1	4	4	4	13	2	74	2	10	0	67	163
CO	Colorado	8	1	2	15	26	3	5	0	2	3	3	16	3	35	5	13	2	107	157
CT	Connecticut	3	0	2	0	5	5	4	1	1	1	3	3	3	19	1	8	1	59	90
	Yale	2	0	1	6	9	19	5	1	1	1	5	0	3	35	1	12	0	38	100
DC	George Washington	1	2	3	2	7	6	32	2	0	0	6	3	3	51	1	15	2	98	177
	Georgetown	0	2	1	2	5	15	7	6	4	2	8	3	4	45	0	14	0	131	196
	Howard	6	0	1	8	14	4	5	1	0	5	2	1	5	18	0	70	0	11	112
FL	Central Florida	0	4	2	12	16	4	11	0	1	2	2	3	3	26	2	6	0	74	100
	FIU-Wertheim	0	19	0	7	26	8	14	3	2	1	2	2	5	35	0	9	2	77	120
	Florida	0	5	5	10	20	7	8	1	3	0	1	0	4	24	1	12	0	90	132
	Florida Atlantic-Schmidt	1	1	1	6	9	2	1	2	1	0	0	1	2	8	0	2	0	52	63
	Florida State	1	0	2	13	16	3	4	2	3	0	1	0	3	13	1	16	0	88	120
	Miami-Miller	7	17	1	6	25	7	29	3	2	2	0	3	6	47	0	10	0	132	196
	USF-Morsani	0	8	5	13	23	7	17	2	3	0	2	3	3	34	2	13	0	114	163
GA	Emory	1	0	1	2	4	10	13	3	3	0	6	4	3	36	0	13	1	81	135
	MC Georgia	3	0	1	7	11	16	23	5	1	2	11	4	4	63	3	11	0	147	230
	Mercer	1	0	0	2	3	0	12	2	1	0	2	1	1	18	0	4	0	75	99
	Morehouse	1	0	0	6	7	3	7	1	5	0	4	3	4	21	1	32	1	10	64
HI	Hawaii-Burns	0	0	0	1	1	22	0	0	0	24	7	4	1	50	0	1	5	16	66
IA	Iowa-Carver	6	0	3	2	10	6	9	1	0	2	2	2	4	22	3	5	1	122	152
IL	Chicago Med-Franklin	3	1	2	3	8	13	33	10	6	2	11	6	8	86	3	8	0	94	190
	Chicago-Pritzker	4	1	1	0	6	10	10	3	0	1	0	0	1	25	1	9	0	53	88
	Illinois	26	5	5	31	63	31	29	4	7	1	15	3	6	91	5	32	0	184	315
	Loyola-Stritch	6	5	1	6	12	3	1	1	2	0	3	2	2	14	0	12	0	127	157
	Northwestern-Feinberg	4	5	1	5	14	17	18	0	2	0	4	4	5	47	3	11	0	95	161
	Rush	4	2	2	9	16	7	13	2	3	1	3	4	0	29	3	8	2	88	128
	Southern Illinois	3	0	1	1	3	3	2	0	2	1	0	1	0	9	0	7	0	54	72
IN	Indiana	11	1	2	4	18	20	17	3	6	3	3	3	8	62	1	27	1	245	335
KS	Kansas	8	0	0	4	11	6	5	1	2	2	1	2	7	26	3	13	0	173	211
KY	Kentucky	0	1	0	0	0	6	2	1	2	0	1	0	4	15	0	5	0	86	118
	Louisville	1	1	0	3	4	2	6	2	3	1	1	1	1	17	0	7	0	132	155
LA	LSU New Orleans	1	1	0	4	6	7	9	3	3	0	2	8	2	32	0	9	0	145	190
	LSU Shreveport	1	1	2	4	8	3	4	1	0	1	0	2	0	10	0	9	1	101	119
	Tulane	2	0	0	4	6	14	9	0	0	1	5	6	2	34	0	9	0	140	188

Source: AAMC: Data Warehouse: Applicant Matriculant File as of 10/9/2012. *Hispanic Ethnicities are alone or in combination with some other Hispanic Ethnicity and include any Race. Ethnicity Counts include U.S. Citizens and Permanent Residents only. Race Counts include U.S. Citizens and Permanent Residents only, are alone or in combination with some other Race, and include both Hispanic and Non-Hispanic Ethnicity. The total represents an unduplicated count and also includes matriculants for whom we have no race data or who are foreign...

Table 8-A:
Matriculants by Medical School and Race and Ethnicity 2012* (continued)

	School	Mexican American	Cuban	Puerto Rican	Other Hispanic or Latino	Total Hispanic or Latino	Chinese	Asian Indian	Pakistani	Filipino	Japanese	Korean	Vietnamese	Other Asian	Total Asian	Native American (incl AK)	Black	Native Hawaiian /OPI	White	Unduplicated
MA	Boston	6	7	5	14	29	18	25	2	1	2	8	2	5	62	0	10	0	88	181
	Harvard	6	3	1	6	15	17	14	2	0	0	5	2	4	42	4	14	0	88	164
	Massachusetts	1	0	3	4	7	10	12	2	0	0	1	2	4	29	2	6	0	92	125
	Tufts	5	1	4	6	14	18	13	0	3	3	6	3	2	48	1	12	1	141	200
MD	Johns Hopkins	4	2	1	5	10	13	8	3	0	2	1	1	5	32	2	14	0	67	119
	Maryland	0	1	0	3	4	23	14	1	3	0	5	1	4	49	1	7	0	101	160
	Uniformed Services-Hebert	2	1	0	2	5	11	3	0	3	1	11	1	5	32	0	7	1	132	171
MI	Michigan	2	2	2	6	10	16	15	3	1	2	4	1	1	43	1	8	1	129	177
	Michigan State	8	1	1	6	15	16	11	2	4	2	5	6	6	47	2	9	2	142	200
	Oakland Beaumont	0	0	1	3	4	2	6	0	1	1	3	1	0	14	0	4	0	54	75
	Wayne State	4	0	0	1	5	17	24	2	1	1	5	0	10	59	0	11	0	200	290
MN	Mayo	2	0	0	1	3	4	5	1	0	1	3	1	2	15	0	2	0	26	50
	Minnesota	2	0	0	3	5	9	8	0	0	1	5	2	2	26	9	7	1	187	230
MO	Missouri Columbia	0	0	0	1	1	2	0	1	1	0	0	1	2	8	2	4	0	82	96
	Missouri Kansas City	0	0	0	2	2	0	3	0	0	0	0	2	43	48	0	8	0	40	110
	St Louis	3	0	0	4	7	20	24	0	2	0	4	2	6	55	0	9	0	100	178
	Washington U St Louis	4	0	1	3	8	20	11	0	1	1	3	0	2	37	1	6	0	69	124
MS	Mississippi	0	0	0	0	0	2	4	0	3	0	1	0	2	12	0	15	0	107	135
NC	Duke	1	1	0	2	4	15	15	1	0	0	0	1	1	33	0	10	0	53	101
	East Carolina-Brody	0	0	1	2	2	2	4	0	1	0	1	1	1	11	1	9	0	59	80
	North Carolina	3	2	3	6	14	5	11	0	2	1	1	2	2	22	3	22	0	132	180
	Wake Forest	2	1	0	1	4	7	7	0	0	0	1	2	0	17	1	17	1	86	120
ND	North Dakota	0	0	0	0	0	0	2	0	1	0	0	0	1	4	7	0	0	61	70
NE	Creighton	2	0	0	5	6	12	4	0	3	5	4	4	1	27	1	2	1	121	152
	Nebraska	1	0	0	0	1	3	0	2	0	0	2	1	0	6	1	1	1	117	129
NH	Dartmouth-Geisel	2	0	2	6	10	9	5	1	0	0	2	0	2	18	4	7	0	48	87
NJ	Cooper Rowan	0	2	1	3	6	2	3	1	2	0	1	0	1	10	1	5	0	31	50
	UMDNJ New Jersey	2	2	3	14	21	22	40	4	5	0	9	0	4	81	2	18	1	68	178
	UMDNJ-RW Johnson	1	1	4	7	10	8	19	1	0	1	5	1	3	37	0	10	0	76	134
NM	New Mexico	16	0	0	14	29	1	2	0	0	0	1	2	0	5	9	2	1	77	103
NV	Nevada	5	1	1	4	11	5	2	2	2	1	3	0	2	14	2	2	0	52	68
NY	Albany	5	0	4	1	9	12	17	2	2	1	6	2	7	50	1	7	0	83	138
	Buffalo	1	1	0	1	3	16	5	1	0	1	6	1	1	30	1	7	0	107	144
	Columbia	5	2	3	7	17	13	3	0	0	1	0	1	4	20	1	17	0	116	166
	Cornell-Weill	1	2	1	8	12	11	8	0	0	1	6	1	0	27	2	7	1	55	101
	Einstein	1	0	0	6	7	25	9	3	2	1	8	1	6	55	2	11	1	99	183
	Hofstra North Shore-LIJ	0	1	0	4	6	9	3	0	0	0	1	1	0	14	1	2	1	46	60
	Mount Sinai	3	2	1	12	16	9	9	0	0	0	5	0	4	28	1	9	0	81	139
	New York Medical	2	3	2	8	13	25	8	4	1	2	1	4	3	44	0	19	0	127	195
	New York University	2	2	1	9	14	22	14	5	1	2	9	2	6	59	1	2	3	86	158
	Rochester	1	0	1	4	6	8	4	0	0	1	3	2	3	21	1	9	1	69	102
	SUNY Downstate	0	2	3	2	7	26	21	3	2	1	7	4	0	68	1	25	0	85	185
	SUNY Upstate	2	0	1	5	7	10	7	3	1	0	4	1	2	28	1	13	0	101	156
	Stony Brook	0	1	3	3	7	20	11	1	0	0	5	4	4	45	0	7	0	71	124
OH	Case Western	8	4	2	5	18	24	26	0	4	1	6	0	3	63	1	14	2	101	198
	Cincinnati	0	0	2	3	5	11	9	3	0	0	1	0	7	28	1	11	1	129	171
	Northeast Ohio	1	0	0	1	2	9	27	2	1	1	1	1	5	45	0	3	0	83	135
	Ohio State	10	2	2	7	20	25	24	0	1	1	5	2	1	58	1	11	0	99	178
	Toledo	0	0	0	3	3	17	27	2	1	2	5	5	5	57	0	5	0	119	177
	Wright State-Boonshoft	1	0	0	1	2	3	6	0	0	0	2	1	1	14	1	8	1	80	103

Source: AAMC: Data Warehouse: Applicant Matriculant File as of 10/9/2012. *Hispanic Ethnicities are alone or in combination with some other Hispanic Ethnicity and include any Race. Ethnicity Counts include U.S. Citizens and Permanent Residents only. Race Counts include U.S. Citizens and Permanent Residents only, are alone or in combination with some other Race, and include both Hispanic and Non-Hispanic Ethnicity. The total represents an unduplicated count and also includes matriculants for whom we have no race data or who are foreign..

Table 8-A:

Matriculants by Medical School and Race and Ethnicity 2012* (continued)

	School	Mexican American	Cuban	Puerto Rican	Other Hispanic or Latino	Total Hispanic or Latino	Chinese	Asian Indian	Pakistani	Filipino	Japanese	Korean	Vietnamese	Other Asian	Total Asian	Native American (incl AK)	Black	Native Hawaiian /OPI	White	Unduplicated
OK	Oklahoma	1	0	0	1	2	11	12	1	3	2	1	10	1	39	8	2	0	118	161
OR	Oregon	4	0	0	2	6	9	2	1	0	1	2	3	1	18	2	1	0	112	132
PA	Commonwealth	0	2	1	2	4	3	9	1	1	0	4	2	2	20	0	6	0	44	70
	Drexel	3	1	2	8	14	25	36	5	3	0	14	4	10	94	0	18	0	140	260
	Jefferson	1	1	2	8	12	16	24	1	1	1	2	4	5	51	2	5	1	179	260
	Penn State	3	0	0	3	6	8	6	2	1	0	5	0	2	23	1	8	0	107	145
	Pennsylvania-Perelman	2	3	4	8	17	17	11	1	1	0	4	1	3	38	2	20	0	106	163
	Pittsburgh	0	4	2	3	8	20	17	3	0	1	5	3	2	51	1	14	0	75	145
	Temple	4	8	3	10	22	11	21	1	1	1	9	4	1	49	1	12	0	148	207
PR	Caribe	0	3	51	6	57	1	1	0	0	0	0	0	1	4	0	9	0	40	65
	Ponce	2	2	60	7	66	0	0	1	0	0	0	0	0	1	0	7	0	50	70
	Puerto Rico	0	0	105	4	107	0	0	0	0	0	0	0	0	0	0	11	0	88	110
RI	San Juan Bautista	3	5	36	12	53	0	0	0	0	0	0	0	0	0	0	8	0	48	59
	Brown-Alpert	3	2	2	5	12	13	10	2	2	1	4	1	4	36	0	12	0	57	120
SC	MU South Carolina	1	0	2	7	10	3	8	1	1	2	1	1	1	18	0	23	0	129	168
	South Carolina	0	0	0	1	1	3	5	0	0	0	0	1	0	9	0	11	1	71	94
	South Carolina Greenville	0	0	0	3	3	0	1	1	0	0	0	0	0	2	1	4	0	45	53
SD	South Dakota-Sanford	0	0	0	1	1	2	0	0	0	1	1	0	0	4	0	0	0	52	58
TN	East Tennessee-Quillen	0	1	1	0	1	0	2	0	0	0	1	1	1	4	1	0	0	66	72
	Meharry	3	0	0	2	5	2	2	0	1	1	1	0	3	8	0	82	0	10	105
	Tennessee	1	1	0	2	4	6	7	1	0	1	4	0	4	20	0	12	0	128	165
	Vanderbilt	1	3	1	10	15	9	5	2	0	0	0	0	3	19	3	11	0	73	105
TX	Baylor	9	0	1	6	16	26	23	9	2	0	2	10	4	72	3	13	0	96	185
	Texas A & M	9	0	1	20	30	8	13	5	3	0	1	5	27	62	3	9	0	119	200
	Texas Tech	5	0	0	11	16	9	11	1	1	0	2	6	28	55	2	2	0	88	150
	Texas Tech-Foster	3	1	0	10	12	2	4	0	1	0	2	3	14	25	0	1	0	53	79
	UT Galveston	4	0	0	30	34	4	6	3	4	1	3	2	17	39	1	42	0	134	230
	UT HSC San Antonio	10	0	0	39	49	9	6	1	2	0	1	3	14	36	0	9	1	158	213
	UT Houston	6	1	1	27	34	8	18	2	4	1	3	6	15	52	2	16	0	163	240
	UT Southwestern	7	2	1	8	18	34	32	4	2	2	9	5	18	102	0	13	0	111	230
UT	Utah	0	0	0	5	5	2	3	0	1	3	0	3	0	11	0	0	0	74	82
VA	Eastern Virginia	4	0	0	1	5	4	15	4	5	0	4	3	4	38	1	12	0	89	146
	Virginia	1	5	2	11	17	13	11	0	1	1	5	4	3	38	2	6	0	103	156
	Virginia Commonwealth	0	2	1	6	9	7	27	8	3	1	3	8	8	63	0	10	0	126	200
	Virginia Tech Carilion	0	0	0	0	0	2	6	0	0	0	2	1	0	11	0	0	0	30	42
VT	Vermont	2	0	0	8	10	9	8	0	2	2	4	2	6	31	0	3	0	73	112
WA	U Washington	7	1	1	2	10	9	4	2	3	4	6	3	2	30	0	3	3	185	220
WI	MC Wisconsin	11	0	1	2	13	17	3	0	1	3	3	4	2	30	7	15	0	158	204
	Wisconsin	3	0	0	2	6	2	4	0	0	0	2	3	6	17	2	13	0	139	175
WV	Marshall-Edwards	1	0	1	1	3	1	2	0	0	0	0	2	0	3	0	1	0	60	66
	West Virginia	0	0	0	1	2	1	7	0	0	1	1	0	0	13	0	4	0	86	106
	Totals	451	181	403	778	1,731	1,420	1,422	210	211	158	470	330	572	4,572	184	1,416	52	12,773	19,517

Source: AAMC: Data Warehouse: Applicant Matriculant File as of 10/9/2012. *Hispanic Ethnicities are alone or in combination with some other Hispanic Ethnicity and include any Race. Ethnicity Counts include U.S. Citizens and Permanent Residents only. Race Counts include U.S. Citizens and Permanent Residents only, are alone or in combination with some other Race, and include both Hispanic and Non-Hispanic Ethnicity. The total represents an unduplicated count and also includes matriculants for whom we have no race data or who are foreign..

CHAPTER 9:
Be in the Know: AAMC Recommendations for Medical School Admission Officers

What follows are a set of recommendations for medical school application, acceptance, and admission procedures that all of our members have agreed to follow. We share them with you here because it is important you be aware of these procedures as they relate to your own application, ensuring that these processes are timely and fair for all concerned.

These recommendations correspond directly to the AAMC Recommendations for Applicants in Chapter 6

The AAMC recommends that:

1. Each school:
   a. Publish annually, amend publicly, and adhere to its application, acceptance, and admission procedures.

   b. Utilizing an application service, abide by all conditions of its participation agreement with that application service.

2. Each school:
   a. Between August 1 and March 15, notify the AAMC Section for Medical School Application Services of all admission actions within four weeks of those actions being taken.

   b. Between March 16 and the first day of class, notify the AAMC Section for Medical School Application Services of all admission actions within seven days of those actions being taken.

3. Each school notify all applicants—other than Combined College/M.D., Early Decision Program (EDP), and deferred matriculation applicants—of acceptance to medical school only after October 15 of each admission cycle. It may be appropriate to communicate notifications of decisions other than acceptance to medical school to applicants prior to October 15.

4. By March 30 of the matriculation year, March 15 for M.D.-Ph.D. programs, each school or program have issued a number of offers of acceptance at least equal to the expected number of students in its first-year entering class and have reported those acceptance actions to the AAMC Section for Medical School Application Services.

continued...

5. Prior to May 15 of the matriculation year (April 15 for schools whose first day of class is on or before July 30), April 30 for M.D.-Ph.D. programs, each school or program permit ALL applicants (except for EDP applicants)—including those to whom merit or other special scholarships have been awarded:

   a. A minimum two-week time period for their response to the acceptance offer.

   b. To hold acceptance offers from any other schools or programs without penalty.

6. After May 15 of the matriculation year (April 15 for schools whose first day of class is on or before July 30), April 30 for M.D.-Ph.D. programs, each school or program implement school-specific procedures for accepted applicants who, without adequate explanation, continue to hold one or more places at other schools or programs. These procedures:

   a. May require applicants to:

      i. Respond to acceptance offers in less than two weeks.

      ii. Submit a statement of intent, a deposit, or both.

   b. Should recognize the problems of applicants with multiple acceptance offers, applicants who have not yet received an acceptance offer, and applicants who have not yet been informed about financial aid opportunities at schools to which they have been accepted.

   c. Should permit accepted applicants to remain on other schools' or programs' waiting lists and to withdraw if they later receive an acceptance offer from a preferred school or program.

7. Each school's acceptance deposit not exceed $100 and (except for EDP applicants) be refundable until May 15, April 30 for M.D.-Ph.D. applicants. If the applicant enrolls at the school, the school is encouraged to credit the deposit toward tuition.

8. After June 1, May 15 for M.D.-Ph.D. programs, any school that plans to make an acceptance offer to an applicant already known to have been accepted by another school or program for that entering class ensure that the other school or program is advised of this offer at the time that the offer is made. This notification should be made immediately by telephone and promptly thereafter by written correspondence delivered by regular or electronic methods. Schools and programs should communicate fully with each other with respect to anticipated late roster changes in order to minimize inter-school miscommunication and misunderstanding, as well as the possibility of unintended vacant positions in a school's first-year entering class.

9. No school make an acceptance offer, either verbal or written, to any individual who has enrolled in, or begun an orientation program immediately prior to enrollment at, a U.S. or Canadian school. Enrollment is defined as being officially matriculated as a member of the school's first-year class.

10. Each school treats all letters of evaluation submitted in support of an application as confidential, except in those states with applicable laws to the contrary. The contents of a letter of recommendation should not be revealed to an applicant at any time.

Approved: AAMC Council of Deans Administrative Board, February 17, 2009

CHAPTER 10:
Applicant and Acceptee Data

Up until this point, we've touched upon a wide range of topics related to acceptance to medical school—including undergraduate preparation, the MCAT® exam, choosing a school, the application process, and the factors that enter into the admissions decision. We now turn to two additional questions that are likely at the very top of your mind:

Who applies to medical school…and who gets in?

We realize, of course, that the question you're really asking is "based on my numbers, will I get in?" We can't tell you. What we can do, however, is provide you with data related to last year's applicants—both those who were accepted and those who were not—so that you can determine your relative standing on a variety of admissions-related factors. With your advisor's help, this information will enable you to make appropriate decisions related to your application to medical school. Extensive information about medical school applicants and matriculants can also be found at www.aamc.org/facts.

A Quick Look at the 2012 Entering Class

- In 2011–12, 45,266 people applied to the 2012 entering class at all M.D.-granting medical schools in the United States.

- By the fall of 2012, 20,479 applicants had been offered an acceptance to at least one medical school, and 19,517 accepted applicants had matriculated.

These accepted applicants possessed a broad range of MCAT® scores and undergraduate grade point averages, and a wide variety of personal characteristics and life experiences. Both male and female applicants were distributed across numerous racial and ethnic groups. A small number applied through the Early Decision Program, but the majority used the regular application process. A small number of accepted applicants chose not to matriculate in 2012.

This chapter contains graphic representations of relevant data for the entire applicant pool, as well as for accepted and not accepted applicants, for the 2012 entering class. All data presented in this chapter are accurate as of October 9, 2012*. In the following charts:

- "All applicants" refers to all applicants to the 2012 entering class

- "Accepted applicants" refers to those applicants accepted to at least one medical school

- "Not accepted applicants" refers to those applicants not accepted to any medical school

In the following pages, we provide data related to performance on the MCAT® exam, undergraduate grade point average, MCAT® scores and undergraduate GPA combined, undergraduate major, gender, age, type of application, and race and ethnicity.

*Source: AAMC DataWarehouse; Applicant Matriculant File

Performance on the MCAT exam

Charts 10-A—10-E present information about the performance of applicants on the MCAT® exam:

- **Chart 10-A** shows that applicants achieved Verbal Reasoning (VR) scores at each score from 1 to 15; the largest number achieved a VR score of 10. Accepted applicants' scores ranged from 2 to 15, although very few had VR scores below 5 (just over 80). At a VR score of 10, the number of accepted applicants exceeded the number not accepted.

- **Chart 10-B** shows that applicants achieved Physical Sciences (PS) scores at each score from 1 to 15; the largest number achieved a PS score of 10. Accepted applicants' scores ranged from 3 to 15; just over 50 accepted applicants achieved a score of 5 or below. Accepted applicants exceeded not accepted applicants at a PS score of 10.

Chart 10-A

MCAT® Verbal Reasoning Score Distribution, Year 2012 Applicants

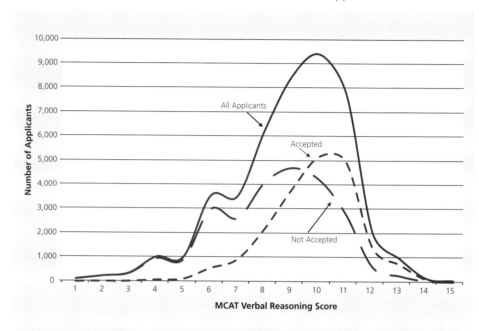

Source: AAMC Data Warehouse: Applicant Matriculant File

As of October 9, 2012

*The new medical schools accredited in 2011 will enroll their first matriculants in 2012.

Chart 10-B

MCAT® Physical Sciences Score Distribution, Year 2012 Applicants

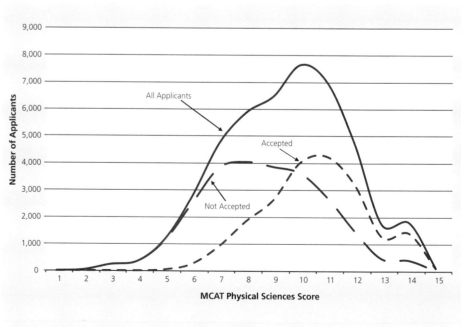

Source: AAMC Data Warehouse: Applicant Matriculant File

As of October 9, 2012

Chart 10-C

MCAT® Writing Sample Score Distribution, Year 2012 Applicants

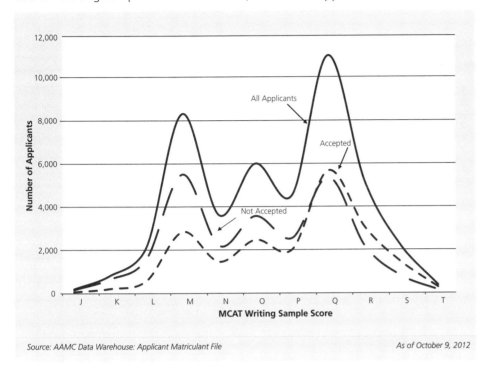

Source: AAMC Data Warehouse: Applicant Matriculant File

As of October 9, 2012

- **Chart 10-C** shows that applicants achieved Writing Sample (WS) scores at each score from J to T; the largest number achieved a WS score of Q. Accepted applicants' scores ranged from J to T; the number with scores of K and below was just over 190. Accepted applicants exceeded not accepted applicants at a score of Q.

- **Chart 10-D** shows that applicants achieved Biological Sciences (BS) scores at each score from 1 to 15; the largest number achieved a BS score of 10. Accepted applicants' scores ranged from 3 to 15; just over 15 scored 5 or below. Accepted applicants exceeded not accepted applicants at a score of 11.

Chart 10-D

MCAT® Biological Sciences Score Distribution, Year 2012 Applicants

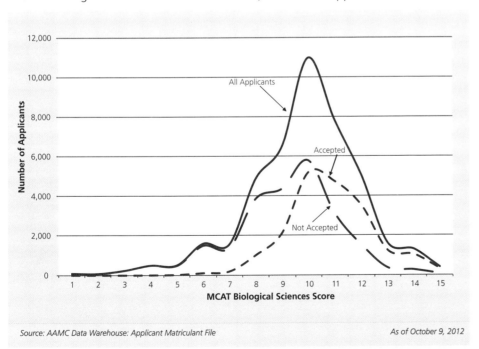

Source: AAMC Data Warehouse: Applicant Matriculant File

As of October 9, 2012

- **Chart 10-E**—which shows total scores on the numerically scored sections of Verbal Reasoning, Physical Sciences, and Biological Sciences—reveals that applicants achieved total scores from 4 to 45; the largest number achieved a total score of 30. Accepted applicants achieved total scores from 10 to 45; the number of accepted applicants with total scores of 17 and below (an average of almost 6 on each section) was just under 20. Accepted applicants exceeded not accepted applicants at a total score of 30.

No score on a single MCAT® section and no total MCAT® score "guarantees" admission to medical school. Charts 10-A, 10-B, and 10-D reveal that, while applicants with VR, PS, and BS scores of 10 and above had a higher probability of being accepted to medical school, a significant number of applicants with such scores were not accepted. The same holds true for the Writing Sample section; a score of Q and above is a likely, though not definite, barometer for acceptance. Finally, Chart 10-E shows that a substantial number of applicants with total MCAT® scores of 30 and above were not accepted. These findings reveal the importance of factors other than MCAT® performance—including undergraduate academic performance and a variety of personal characteristics and experiential variables—in the medical student selection process.

Undergraduate Grade Point Average (GPA)

Charts 10-F—10-H present information about the undergraduate academic performance of applicants:

- **Chart 10-F**: undergraduate science GPA (biology, chemistry, physics, and mathematics)

- **Chart 10-G**: undergraduate non-science GPA

- **Chart 10-H**: undergraduate total GPA

Chart 10-F shows that the undergraduate science GPAs of all

Chart 10-E

MCAT® Total Numeric Score Distribution, Year 2012 Applicants

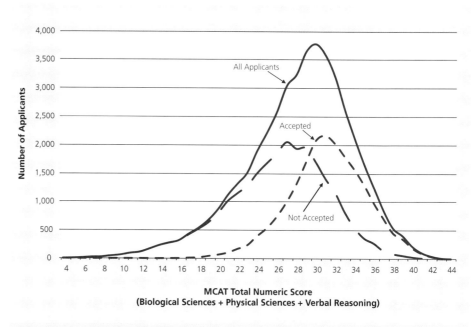

**MCAT Total Numeric Score
(Biological Sciences + Physical Sciences + Verbal Reasoning)**

Source: AAMC Data Warehouse: Applicant Matriculant File

As of October 9, 2012

Chart 10-F

GPA Science Distribution, Year 2012 Applicants

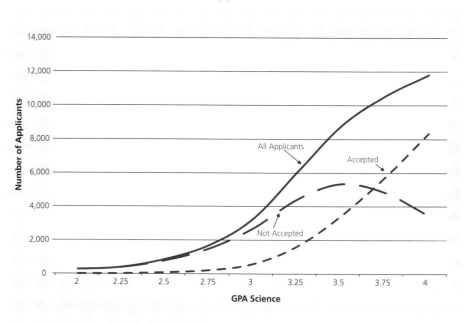

GPA Science

Source: AAMC Data Warehouse: Applicant Matriculant File

As of October 9, 2012

Chart 10-G

GPA Non-Science Distribution, Year 2012 Applicants

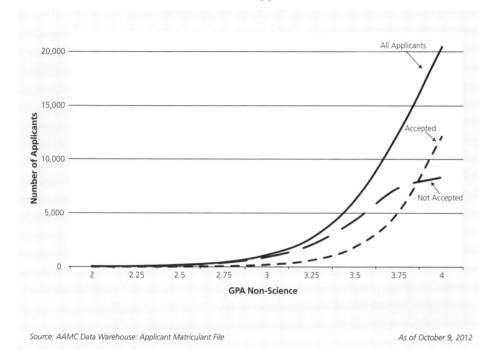

Source: AAMC Data Warehouse: Applicant Matriculant File

As of October 9, 2012

Chart 10-H

GPA Total Distribution, Year 2012 Applicants

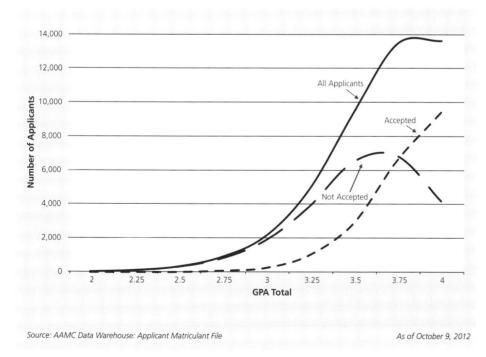

Source: AAMC Data Warehouse: Applicant Matriculant File

As of October 9, 2012

applicants were on a continuum from just under 2.0 to 4.0, on a 4.0 scale; most were between 3.75 and 4.0. Accepted applicants also had undergraduate science GPAs across the entire range, but few had GPAs of 2.50 or below (just over 90). The undergraduate science GPA at which accepted applicants exceeded those not accepted was between 3.50 and 3.75.

Chart 10-G shows applicants' undergraduate non-science GPAs along the continuum from just under 2.0 to 4.0, with most between 3.75 and 4.0. Accepted applicants' undergraduate non-science GPAs also ranged from 2.0 to 4.0, but only about 85 had a GPA of 2.75 or below. At 3.75 to 4.0, accepted applicants exceeded not accepted applicants.

As shown in **Chart 10-H**, all applicants had total undergraduate GPAs from just under 2.0 to 4.0, and most were in the range of 3.50 to 3.75. Accepted applicants' total undergraduate GPAs ranged from 2.0 to 4.0, but just over 105 possessed undergraduate total GPAs of 2.75 or below. Accepted applicants exceeded not accepted applicants at an undergraduate total GPA of between 3.75 and 4.0.

As is the case with MCAT® data, GPA data in Charts 10-F–10-H show that no undergraduate GPA assures admission to medical school. While applicants with undergraduate science, nonscience, and total GPAs in the range of 3.50 to 3.75, 3.75 to 4.0, and 3.75 to 4.0, respectively, were more likely to be accepted to medical school, a significant number of such applicants were not accepted. Again, these findings underscore the importance of a wide variety of personal characteristics and experiential variables in the medical student selection process.

MCAT® and Undergraduate GPA

Chart 10-I combines MCAT® scores and undergraduate GPA for all applicants to medical school from 2010 to 2012. The data may not reflect your particular circumstances. As a result, we recommend that you go to *www.aamc.org/facts* to see acceptance rates for particular demographic groups. Note that these results are presented without regard to any of the other selection factors.

Chart 10-I
MCAT® and Undergraduate GPA Combined

GPA Total		MCAT® Total									
		4-14	15-17	18-20	21-23	24-26	27-29	30-32	33-35	36-38	39-45
3.80-4.00	Acceptees	2	8	80	336	1,376	4,126	6,536	5,552	3,150	1,255
	Applicants	80	176	517	1,408	3,401	6,334	8,134	6,444	3,500	1,377
	Accs/Apps	2.5%	4.5%	15.5%	23.9%	40.5%	65.1%	80.4%	86.2%	90.0%	91.1%
3.60-3.79	Acceptees	0	12	99	387	1,223	3,724	5,763	4,108	1,647	372
	Applicants	167	3802	1,006	2,220	4,580	7,622	8,239	5,211	1,999	446
	Accs/Apps	0.0%	3.1%	9.8%	17.4%	26.7%	48.9%	69.9%	78.8%	82.4%	83.4%
3.40-3.59	Acceptees	2	18	95	383	1,038	2,371	3,539	2,285	799	188
	Applicants	301	529	1,204	2,541	4,557	6,808	6,804	3,496	1,122	236
	Accs/Apps	0.7%	3.4%	7.9%	15.1%	22.8%	34.8%	52.0%	65.4%	71.2%	79.7%
3.20-3.39	Acceptees	1	9	74	258	612	1,051	1463	891	333	70
	Applicants	318	513	1099	2,060	3,260	4,257	3,876	1,793	527	107
	Accs/Apps	0.3%	1.8%	6.7%	12.5%	18.8%	24.7%	37.7%	49.7%	63.2%	65.4%
3.00-3.19	Acceptees	1	13	49	155	329	530	530	331	97	19
	Applicants	407	484	948	1,479	2,007	2,247	1,766	777	206	33
	Accs/Apps	0.2%	2.7%	5.2%	10.5%	16.4%	23.6%	30.0%	42.6%	47.1%	57.6%
2.80-2.99	Acceptees	0	4	25	72	151	144	174	86	29	11
	Applicants	341	394	631	814	1010	976	745	274	87	24
	Accs/Apps	0.0%	1.0%	4.0%	8.8%	15.0%	14.8%	23.4%	31.4%	33.3%	45.8%
2.60-2.79	Acceptees	0	3	13	28	53	66	71	32	13	2
	Applicants	273	275	343	443	485	421	297	113	37	11
	Accs/Apps	0.0%	1.1%	3.8%	6.3%	10.9%	15.7%	23.9%	28.3%	35.1%	18.2%
2.40-2.59	Acceptees	0	0	2	6	17	21	23	9	3	0
	Applicants	184	144	179	208	225	157	105	47	17	2
	Accs/Apps	0.0%	0.0%	1.1%	2.9%	7.6%	13.4%	21.9%	19.1%	17.6%	0.0%
2.40-2.59	Acceptees	0	0	2	2	9	7	0	2	0	0
	Applicants	137	61	90	71	77	61	27	14	3	2
	Accs/Apps	0.0%	0.0%	2.2%	2.8%	11.7%	11.5%	0.0%	14.3%	0.0%	0.0%
2.00-2.19	Acceptees	0	0	0	0	1	1	2	0	0	0
	Applicants	64	45	39	28	27	15	17	2	0	1
	Accs/Apps	0.0%	0.0%	0.0%	0.0%	3.7%	6.7%	11.8%	0.0%	--	0.0%
1.20-1.99	Acceptees	0	0	0	0	1	0	0	0	0	0
	Applicants	44	13	10	7	6	10	7	1	0	0
	Accs/Apps	0.0%	0.0%	0.0%	0.0%	16.7%	0.0%	0.0%	0.0%	--	--

Percent Accepted = ■ 25% – 49%   ■ 50% – 74%   ■ 75% – 100%

Source: AAMC Data Warehouse: Applicant Matriculant File

As of October 9, 2012

Chart 10-J

Undergraduate Major Distribution, All Applicants, 2008–2012

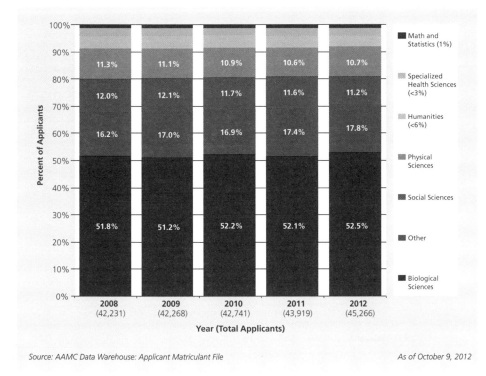

Source: AAMC Data Warehouse: Applicant Matriculant File

As of October 9, 2012

Chart 10-J presents information about the undergraduate majors of all medical school applicants to the 2008-2012 entering classes. Over the past five years, more than half of all applicants reported undergraduate biological science majors, while the remainder reported a variety of majors, including the humanities, mathematics and statistics, physical sciences, social sciences, other health sciences, and a broad "other" category. The proportion of these majors has remained relatively constant over time, despite annual fluctuations in the applicant pool.

Chart 10-K presents similar information about the undergraduate majors of applicants accepted to the 2008-2012 entering classes. Comparisons of the majors of the total applicant pool with those of accepted applicants reveal acceptance rates, for various science-related majors, ranging from 34.8 percent for applicants with specialized health science majors, to 44.0 percent for biological science majors, to 51.3 percent for physical science majors, the highest rate of acceptance for science-related majors.

Chart 10-K

Undergraduate Major Distribution, Accepted Applicants, 2008–2012

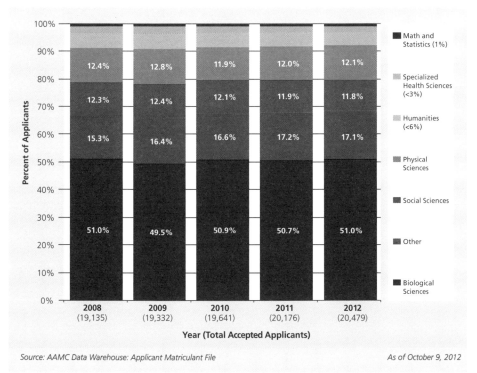

Source: AAMC Data Warehouse: Applicant Matriculant File

As of October 9, 2012

Gender

Chart 10-L presents information about the number and gender of the entire applicant pool and of accepted applicants for the 1992-2012 entering classes. The largest annual applicant pool during the past 20 years was for the 1996 entering class; since that year, the pool gradually declined until 2003, when there was a slight increase (3.5 percent) in applicants. The applicant pool increased again by 2.7 percent in 2004, by 4.6 percent in 2005, by another 4.6 percent in 2006, and by 8.2 percent in 2007. In 2008 and 2009, the applicant pool held relatively steady, with a slight decrease of 0.2 percent from 2007 to 2008 and a slight increase of 0.1 percent from 2008 to 2009. In 2012, the applicant pool increased 3.1 percent from 2011. The number of male applicants to the 2012 entering class increased by 1,203 from the number of male applicants to the previous year's entering class, but that number was still smaller than it had been for any other entering class from 1993 through 1997. The number of female applicants to the 2012 class increased by 142 over the number of female applicants to the previous year's entering class, the year 2012 being the largest number of female applicants on record. While the number of accepted applicants remained fairly constant for 10 years, it has started to increase in recent years, from a low of 17,312 in 1997 to a high of 20,479 in 2012. The number of accepted male applicants has fluctuated from a low of 8,810 in 2003 to a high of 10,964 in 2012. The number of accepted female applicants has increased, with small fluctuations, from a low of 7,255 in the 1994 entering class to

Chart 10-L

Applicants by Gender and Acceptance Status, 1992–2012

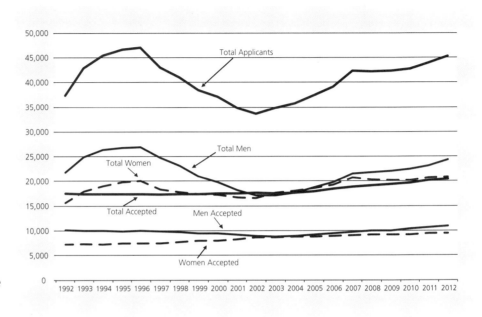

Source: AAMC Data Warehouse: Applicant Matriculant File

As of October 9, 2012

a high of 9,514 in 2012. The significant gaps between male and female applicants for the 1992 entering class (6,166) and the 1993 entering class (6,892) have lessened; 553 and 301 more women than men applied to the 2003 and 2004 entering classes, respectively. In 2005, only 121 more men than women applied. In 2012, 3,416 more men than women applied to medical school. During the same time span, the gaps between accepted male and accepted female applicants also dropped. Accepted male applicants outnumbered accepted female applicants by 2,951 for the 1992 entering class, but only by 1,450 for the 2012 entering class. The national ratio of male to female applicants was 49.2: 50.8 percent for the 2003 entering class, the first time that the number of female applicants was greater than the number of male applicants to medical school. For the 2004 entering class, this trend continued, with a ratio of male to female applicants of 49.6 : 50.4. For the 2005 entering class, there were once again more male than female applicants, with a ratio of male to female applicants of 50.2 : 49.8. This trend continued in 2012, with a ratio of male to female applicants of 53.8 : 46.2.

Chart 10-M

Age Distribution, Year 2012 Applicants

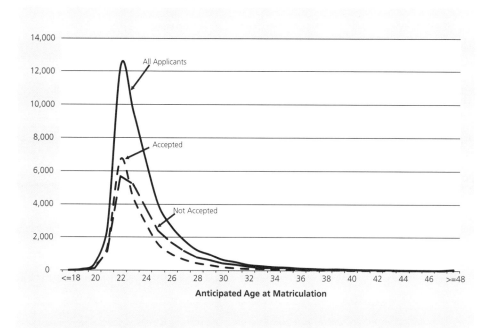

Source: AAMC Data Warehouse: Applicant Matriculant File

As of October 9, 2012

Chart 10-N

Percent of Applicants and Accepted Applicants Reporting Selected Experiences

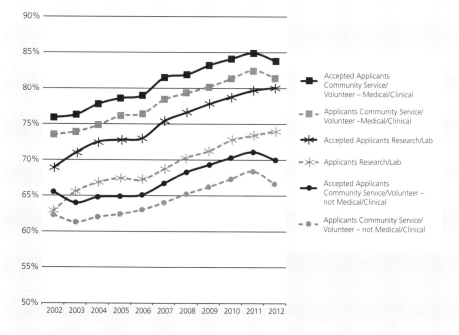

Source: AAMC Data Warehouse: Applicant Matriculant File

As of October 9, 2012

Age

Chart 10-M shows that the age distribution for all applicants to the 2012 entering class was broad, with 22 applicants under the age of 19 at the time of anticipated matriculation, and 68 applicants aged 48 and over. The largest contingent of applicants, 40,865, was between 21 and 28 at the time of anticipated matriculation; the rest of the applicant pool were either under 21 (476) or over 28 (3,925) at the time of anticipated matriculation. Chart 10-M illustrates a similar finding for accepted applicants. Accepted applicants for the 2012 entering class were between 17 and 53 years of age at the time of expected matriculation.

Applicant and Accepted Applicant Experiences

Chart 10-N presents information regarding the volunteer, paid, and lab experiences of AMCAS applicants and accepted applicants to the 2012 entering class. The chart clearly shows the steady increase in both applicants and accepted applicants reporting volunteer medical, community service, and research experience since 2002:

- 84% of accepted applicants reported medical/clinical community service/volunteer clinical experience, an increase of about 8% since 2002

- 81% of applicants reported medical/clinical community service/volunteer clinical experience, an increase of about 8% since 2002

- 80% of accepted applicants reported research/lab experience, an increase of about 11% since 2002

- 74% of applicants reported research/lab experience, an increase of about 11% since 2002

- 70% of accepted applicants reported non-medical/non-clinical community service/volunteer clinical experience, an increase of about 4% since 2002

- 67% of applicants reported non-medical/non-clinical community service/volunteer clinical experience, an increase of about 4% since 2002

The rising trend in reported experiences among applicants and accepted applicants is expected to continue in the coming years.

Race and Ethnicity

Chart 10-O shows applicant self-reported race and ethnicity data for all applicants to the 2008 through 2012 entering classes. The following changes occurred in the self-reported racial and ethnic make-up of the applicant pool from 2011 to 2012:

- The number of self-described white applicants in 2011 was 23,958; the number of white applicants in 2012 was 24,342, an increase of 1.6 percent.

- The number of self-described Asian applicants in 2011 was 8,941; the number of Asian applicants in 2012 was 9,427 an increase of 5.4 percent.

- The number of self-described black applicants in 2011 was 3,215; the number of black applicants in 2012 was 3,304, an increase of 2.8 percent.

- The number of self-described Hispanic applicants in 2011 was 3,459; the number of Hispanic applicants in 2012 was 3,701, an increase of 7.0 percent.

- The number of applicants in 2011 whose self-description of their race or ethnicity was in some other category was 4,346; the number of applicants in this cohort in 2012 was 4,492, an increase of 3.4 percent from 2011.

Chart 10-O

Distribution of Self-Reported Ethnicity and Race: All Applicants, 2008–2012

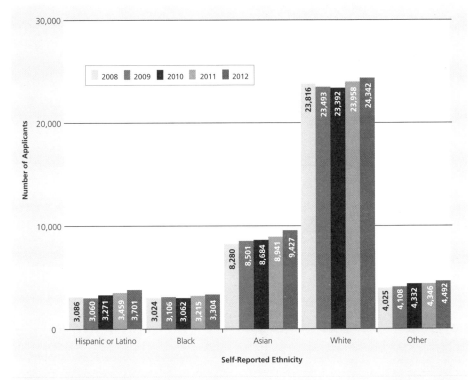

Source: AAMC Data Warehouse: Applicant Matriculant File   As of October 9, 2012

* "Hispanic or Latino Ethnicity" includes all Races; Applicants' Self-Report of only "Black" OR "Asian" OR "White" Race is counted in "Black", "Asian", or "White"; Applicants' Self-Report of Multiple Races is counted in "Other"

Simultaneously, the following changes occurred among those applicants accepted to the 2010 and 2011 entering classes:

- The number of self-described white accepted applicants in 2011 was 11,577; the number of white accepted applicants in 2012 was 11,535, a decrease of 0.4 percent.

- The number of self-described Asian accepted applicants in 2011 was 4,029; the number of accepted Asian applicants in 2012 was 4,243, an increase of 5.3 percent.

- The number of self-described black accepted applicants in 2011 was 1,231; the number of accepted black applicants in 2012 was 1,227, a decrease of 0.3 percent.

- The number of self-described Hispanic accepted applicants in 2011 was 1,701; the number of Hispanic accepted applicants in 2012 was 1,782 an increase of 4.8 percent.

- The number of accepted applicants in 2011 whose self-description of their race or ethnicity was in some other category was 1,638; the number of accepted applicants in this cohort in 2012 was 1,692, an increase of 3.3 percent from 2011.

Additional information of interest to applicants from groups under-represented in medicine is available in Chapter 8.

CHAPTER 11:
Financing Your Medical Education

There's no doubt that medical school is an expensive undertaking, and you'll soon face a myriad of expenses. In addition to the tuition, you'll also have fees, books, equipment, living expenses, medical insurance, and transportation costs to consider.

Fortunately, there's help. In this chapter, we review the various ways you can finance your medical education— from grants and scholarships, to federal student loans, to service commitment programs that provide financial support—as well as informational resources available to help you navigate the process.

Distribution of Total Financial Aid

- Grants with a Service Commitment
- Grants without a Service Commitment
- Loans

Source: 2011-2012 LCME Part I-B Student Financial Aid Questionnaire

Building a Strong Financial Plan

You'll need to develop a strategy to cover the significant costs associated with your education. Tuition and fees top the list, of course, but you'll also need to buy books and equipment, purchase insurance, cover the costs of transportation, and, quite likely, pay for housing and food.

When you look at the figures in the table on the following page, we understand how the financial challenges that face you might seem overwhelming. Annual tuition, fees, and health insurance* at state medical schools in 2012-2013 averaged approximately $30,532 for state residents and $53,545 for nonresidents; at private schools, the average was $48,297 for residents and $49,897 for nonresidents.

Don't let these numbers discourage you. There's help available.

According to recent surveys conducted by the AAMC, 85 percent of newly graduated M.D.'s have medical school education loans, while 59 percent reported receiving some degree of help through scholarships, stipends, and/or grants (which you don't have to repay). So, it can be done, and it is…by tens of thousands of medical students, every single year.

But first… you'll need a plan.

Source: AAMC Tuition and Fees Survey

Table 11-A

Tuition, Fees and Health Insurance for 2012–2013
First-Year Students in U.S. Medical Schools* (in Dollars)

Private Schools

Student Category	Range	Median	Average
Resident	$19,773 - $59,027	$48,258	$48,320
Nonresident	$32,873 - $59,027	$49,427	$49,927

Public Schools

Student Category	Range	Median	Average
Resident	$16,113 - $45,785	$30,753	$35,032
Nonresident	$22,113 - $78,686	$51,281	$53,545

Analysis excludes East Carolina-Brody, Massachusetts, Mercer, Mississippi, and Southern Illinois. These schools do not accept nonresident medical students, and therefore, they do not report nonresident tuition and fees. Public medical schools excludes Uniformed Services University of Health Sciences which does not charge tuition or student fees.

Source: 2012-2013 AAMC Tuition and Student Fees Questionnaire

By "plan," we mean more than simply learning about the assistance available to you and securing the necessary financing. Before you can get to that vital step, it's important that you understand—and adhere to—the basic principles of successful money management. With that in mind, the two basic recommendations that follow should help you build a strong financial foundation.

Overview: The Financial "Basics"

1. Live Within Your Means

Let's face it. Money will be tight during your medical school years, and a realistic spending plan will be critical to your financial well-being. A well-crafted plan will help you maintain better control of your spending, ensure you cover your essential expenses before making an optional purchase, and prepare for an unexpected expense by building an emergency fund.

Follow some basic principles to create a spending plan to meet your needs. Add up your monthly income, determine your monthly expenses, and calculate the difference. One helpful tip is to categorize your expenses as either "fixed" (ones that stay the same each month, such as rent and insurance premiums) or "variable" (such as groceries and clothing).

From that point, you can then identify areas in which you can scale back (if necessary) to assure that your income and expenses remain in balance. Obvious cost-savings steps include sharing housing expenses with a roommate, buying generic products rather than brand names, preparing more of your meals at home, and taking public transportation or carpooling when possible.

Get Your Financial House in Order

Before you apply for student loans, make sure your "financial house" is in order by:

- Creating a budget
- Paying down deb whenever possible
- Making sure you are current on all outstanding credit obligations

You Can Help Your Credit Score

- Pay your bills on time
- Limit your credit accounts
- Keep balances below your credit limit and pay off debt
- Check your credit report regularly at *www.annualcreditreport.com*

Students with a history of credit problems may not qualify for loans that are based on credit; this includes federal and private loans.

Available Sources of Financing Include...

Grants, Scholarships, and Loan Repayment Programs

- Service Commitment Programs
- Scholarships for Disadvantaged Students
- Loan Repayment/Forgiveness Programs

Loans

- Direct Stafford Loans
- Direct PLUS Loans
- Federal Perkins Loans
- Primary Care Loans
- Loans for Disadvantaged Students

Information on these programs is provided on the following pages.

2. Manage Your Debt Wisely

Given the costs of medical school, it's understandable that the vast majority of medical students borrow money to fund their education—and graduate with a median medical school debt of $160,000. Although the ability to manage debt wisely is important, regardless of one's situation, it becomes even more critical for you—a prospective medical student—when you consider the degree to which you're likely to rely on loans to help pay for your education.

- Be cognizant of the amount you are likely to borrow and be comfortable knowing that your future income will be able to pay for your educational loan debt.

- Educate yourself about various financing options, and keep in mind that your financing opportunities will vary depending upon the school you choose.

- Understand your responsibilities as a borrower. Your primary obligation is to know what loans you hold, the amount of each loan, and the repayment schedule. Beyond that, you must keep your servicers notified of any changes in your name, contact information, or enrollment status.

- Maintain accurate financial aid records, copies of application forms, and any related paperwork.

- Build and maintain a good credit score by meeting your financial obligations. In doing so, you'll strengthen your ability to qualify for and obtain attractive interest rates for credit-based loans, land a job, and rent an apartment. For more information, go to *www.aamc.org/download/78864/data/creditscore.pdf.*

There are an abundance of resources to assist you through this process—including those provided by your pre-health advisor, the pages that follow in this book, and the FIRST program offered by the AAMC.

Types of Financial Aid

How will you pay for medical school?

First, remember that you're not on your own. While the ultimate financial responsibility for your medical education rests with you and your family, there are many resources and tools available to help. The financial aid officer at the medical school will assist you, but you'll also want to talk to your pre-health advisor and familiarize yourself with the Financial Aid Fact Sheets on the AAMC FIRST web site.

Financial aid that is typically available to medical students includes loans, grants, and scholarships.

Loans

It's likely that your funding will come from loans—which, in the case of federal loans, are a form of financial aid. There are a variety of loan programs available to help you finance your education.

Federal loans are generally recommended, and students are advised to apply for these loans before considering private options. The *Loan Programs for Students* table later in this chapter provides specific information about four popular federal student loan programs.

Medical school is expensive, but physicians' salaries are excellent. For example, the median starting salary for a family practice doctor in private practice was $160,000 based on 2011 data, with most other specialties averaging even higher. An investment in medical education is likely to be returned to you many times over.

Grants and Scholarships

When it comes to financing your medical education, the best money is free money, often referred to as "gift aid"—which you don't have to repay.

While grants and scholarships are likely to cover only a portion of your overall educational costs, it's worth noting that many students get some degree of funding from these sources. The source of gift aid can be from the federal government, the state government, other outside offices, and/or your medical school. Your medical school financial aid officer is the best source of information as to which grants and scholarships may be available to you.

The Financial Aid Application Process

The financial aid process varies by institution so you'll need to check with the financial aid officer at each school to determine their requirements. Regardless of the medical school, there's a standard process to apply for federal financial aid.

- **Step 1: Complete the FAFSA**

  Complete and submit the FAFSA form in January—preferably after you've filed your income taxes—filling in both the student and parent* information. The resulting Institutional Student Information Report (ISIR) is sent to your school and determines your financial need. Remember to list your medical school's federal ID code to ensure the results of your FAFSA are sent to your medical school's financial aid office.

- **Step 2: Investigate Sources of Aid**

  Contact the financial aid officer at your medical school to investigate sources of institutional aid as well as to learn about various student loan programs available. To obtain a loan, you'll need to complete a master promissory note (MPN), which is a separate application from the FAFSA.

- **Step 3: Apply Early**

  Complete and return applications as soon as possible. In many cases, programs have limited funds and students who apply early have a better chance of receiving aid. You'd hate to miss out on an offer of financial aid simply because you were late submitting applications.

- **Step 4: Receive and Reply to the Award Letter**

  Once your FAFSA and other required forms are received and processed by your medical school's financial aid office, you'll receive an award letter indicating the types and amounts of financial aid for which you qualify—along with directions for accepting or declining the aid. For more information on award letters, review the Award Letter Fact Sheet: *https://www.aamc.org/download/297592/data/awardletter.pdf*

The Loan Programs for Students table outlines the parameters of four major federal loan programs—Primary Care Loans, Federal Perkins Loans, Direct Stafford Loans, and Direct PLUS Loans. For eligibility and other information, we suggest you talk with the financial aid officer at the medical school you plan to attend.

*Although the FAFSA does not ask for parental information for students working toward a graduate degree, many medical schools require that information for purposes of awarding institutional and/or need-based aid.

Loan Programs for Students

Characteristic	Primary Care Loan	Federal Perkins Loan	Direct Stafford Loan	Direct PLUS Loan
Lender	Medical school financial aid office on behalf of the Department of HHS	Medical school financial aid office on behalf of the federal government	The federal government	The federal government
Based on Need	Yes[1]	Yes	No	No
Citizenship Requirement	U.S. citizen, U.S. national, U.S. permanent resident, or asylum status	U.S. citizen, U.S. national, U.S. permanent resident, or asylum status	U.S. citizen, U.S. national, U.S. permanent resident, or asylum status	U.S. citizen, U.S. national, U.S. permanent resident, or asylum status
Borrowing Limits	Up to cost of attendance (Third- and fourth-year students may receive additional funds to repay previous educational loans received while attending medical school)[2]	$8,000/year $60,000 (undergraduate and graduate combined)	$40,500 - $47,167/year, $224,000 cumulative maximum for premed and medical borrowing[2]	Annual cost of attendance minus other financial aid
Interest Rate	5%	5%	For loans first disbursed after July 1, 2006, 6.8% for life of loan	7.9% for life of loan
Interest subsidy:	While in school, deferment, and during grace period	While in school, deferment, and during grace period	No interest subsidy on Unsubsidized Stafford Loans	No interest subsidy for Direct PLUS Loans
Grace Period	1 year after graduation	9 months after graduation	6 months after graduation	None
Deferments	During school and primary care residency (check your promissory note or ask your financial aid officer)	During school and other deferment periods based on eligibility (check your promissory note or ask your financial aid officer)	During school and other deferment periods based on eligibility (check your promissory note or ask your financial aid officer)	While enrolled at least half-time and for an additional six months after you cease to be enrolled at least half-time.
Repayment Requirements	Minimum: $40/month; 10 to 25 years to repay; Not eligible for loan consolidation	Minimum: $40/month, including interest; maximum 10 years to repay; eligible for loan consolidation	Repayment amounts vary depending upon repayment plan	Repayment amounts vary depending upon repayment plan
Prepayment Penalties	None			
Allowable Cancellations	Death or total and permanent disability			

[1] Borrower must agree upon signing loan agreement to enter and complete a primary care residency and practice in a primary care field, which together must be a total of 10-years in length or until the loan is repaid in full, whichever occurs first. Parent financial information is required for consideration for dependent students.

[2] Both annual and aggregate maximums are subject to change, pending congressional action.

Completing the FAFSA

Many of you are already familiar with the FAFSA—the Free Application for Federal Student Aid—from your undergraduate studies. For those who are not, the FAFSA is the Department of Education's basic form that students must complete and submit before they can be considered for financial aid.

The FAFSA is available in a web-based form at *www.fafsa.ed.gov*. In addition to the form itself, you will also find step-by-step instructions to help complete, submit, and follow up on your application.

Your Financial Aid Package

The financial aid package offered by each medical school to which you've been accepted will be a significant factor when it comes time to deciding which offer you accept. For information on this and other elements you'll want to consider as you decide upon schools, please see Chapter 5.

Financial Aid Principles

When awarding aid, each financial aid office's principles are guided by many factors. The aid package is determined by available institutional resources, family resources available to the student, and the institution's own mission. Additionally, the school compares the cost of attendance and other external variables before making a final determination of aid eligibility.

General Eligibility Criteria

Financial aid programs usually require that the applicant or student is:

- A U.S. citizen, or a permanent resident,
- Making satisfactory academic progress
- In compliance with Selective Service registration requirements

How Medical Schools Determine Eligibility for Financial Aid

Medical Schools are sensitive to the financial needs of their students. Guided by federal regulations, the financial aid officer will determine your cost of attendance by taking into account the following principles:

1. How much does it cost?

The cost of medical education includes the following: tuition, fees, books, supplies, equipment, and living expenses. These components make up the school's Cost of Attendance (COA) and vary by school.

2. What are your resources?

The next area to be considered is the degree to which you can contribute to the overall costs. This amount, called the Expected Family Contribution (EFC), is determined through a need-analysis formula to ensure that all students are treated equitably. Both income and assets are considered.

Even though you are considered to be independent for purposes of federal loans, many institutions require parental financial information to determine eligibility for institutional grants, scholarships, and school-based loans. School officials use this information to assess ability rather than willingness to pay, helping to ensure that certain types of aid are awarded to students with the greatest need.

3. What additional resources are needed?

Finally, the financial aid office will subtract your EFC from the institution's total cost of attendance. The remainder determines how much financial assistance you will require for the upcoming academic year.

The medical school will then send you an "award letter," detailing the amount and type of financial aid it can provide.

You will then be asked to accept or decline the offer—or a portion of it—and return the letter to the school. (The amount of financial aid an institution offers is an important factor in choosing which school to attend. See Chapter 5 for additional information and guidance on making your selection.)

Service Commitment and Loan Forgiveness Programs

There are loan forgiveness and repayment programs available for those interested in reducing their education loan debt through service. These are great options for the person whose career goals align with those of the particular repayment/forgiveness program. These programs vary in structure, requirements, and award amounts. For detailed information about these programs see the information on the following page.

- The federal government provides both service commitment and loan repayment benefits to medical students interested in pursuing careers in primary care and to those who are committed to working in a medically under-served area.

- Individual state programs are available to students and graduates in return for a commitment to serve in the state's areas of need.

- The U.S. Armed Forces have programs that offer support to students enrolled in civilian medical schools in exchange for service in the branch that provided the funding.

For additional details on service commitment and loan forgiveness, please see the AAMC's FIRST Fact Sheets at www.aamc.org/firstfacts.

A Word About Repayment

There are a number of benefits to the federal student loan programs. You don't have to begin repaying the loan until after medical school and residency. There are often interest rate reductions for electronic payment and/or making your payments on time.

There are many repayment options available when it comes time to repay your federal student loans. Your options vary from the Standard Repayment plan where you pay the same amount each month for 10-years to income-driven repayment plans that base your payment on your income.

Your financial aid officer and your loan servicer will provide you with complete information for repayment as you near graduation. For those of you interested in learning more now, please check out the FIRST Fact Sheets on loan repayment choices at www.aamc.org/firstfacts.

A Final Word About Financing Your Medical Education

This chapter is intended to provide you with an overview of the types of available financial aid, the financial aid process, and how eligibility for aid is determined. Please keep in mind that once you have been accepted to medical school, you will work closely with that financial aid officer(s) to determine the requirements for, and specifics of, your financing plan. At this point, take a deep breath and consider your options.

CHAPTER 12:
Information on Combined Undergraduate/M.D. Programs

About one-quarter of U.S. medical schools offer combined college/M.D. programs for graduating high school students. These programs range in length from six to nine years. The first two to four years of the curriculum consist of undergraduate courses, including required premedical courses; the remaining years are devoted to the medical school curriculum. Graduates receive both a bachelor's degree from the undergraduate institution and an M.D. degree from the medical school.

The purposes of these programs vary by institution:

- To permit highly qualified students to plan and complete a broad liberal arts education before initiating their medical studies

- To attract highly capable students to the sponsoring medical school

- To enhance diversity in the educational environment

- To reduce the total number of years required to complete the M.D. degree

- To educate physicians likely to practice in particular geographic areas or to work with medically underserved populations

- To reduce the costs of a medical education

- To prepare physician-scientists and future leaders in health policy

Potential applicants should familiarize themselves with the mission and goals statement of each combined degree program in which they have an interest to ensure a match between their educational and professional goals and those of the program.

These programs typically represent relationships between a medical school and one or more undergraduate colleges located in the same geographic region. They are sometimes part of the same university system, or they can be independent institutions.

Admission is open to highly qualified, mature high school students who are committed to a future career in medicine. State-supported schools generally admit few out-of-state applicants to their combined college/M.D. programs; private schools tend to have greater flexibility regarding state of residency.

While academic requirements vary among the schools sponsoring these programs, they typically include biology, chemistry, physics, English, mathematics, and social science courses. Calculus and foreign-language courses are also frequently required; a computer science course is sometimes recommended. Admission to the medical curriculum may occur immediately or after a student completes a prescribed number of semesters with a minimum grade point average (GPA). In some programs, students are not required to take the MCAT® exam; in other programs, a minimum MCAT® score must be attained for progression through the program.

Progressing through the program from the undergraduate to the medical curriculum is usually contingent on a student's achieving specific criteria in terms of standardized test scores and GPAs and meeting the school's expectations regarding personal and professional behavior.

High school students interested in a combined undergraduate/M.D. program should consult their high school guidance counselor to ensure that they are enrolled in a challenging college preparatory curriculum, one that incorporates the specific courses required for admission to the program. The program descriptions in MSAR Online *www.aamc.org/msar* were compiled from medical schools sponsoring programs of interest to high school students. For additional information, contact each school directly.

View complete, detailed information on each of the combined undergraduate/M.D. programs included in the two lists in this chapter, or in the MSAR® Online web site. For more information about MSAR® Online, a preview of the site and complete list of site features, data and information, see *www.aamc.org/msar.*

List of Medical Schools Offering Combined Undergraduate/M.D. Programs by State, 2014–15

Alabama

University of Alabama School of Medicine

University of South Alabama College of Medicine

California

University of California, San Diego, School of Medicine

Connecticut

University of Connecticut and University of Connecticut School of Medicine

District of Columbia

The George Washington University School of Medicine and Health Sciences and The Columbian School of Arts and Sciences

Howard University College of Medicine

Florida

University of Florida College of Medicine

University of Miami

Illinois

Northwestern University Feinberg School of Medicine

University of Illinois at Chicago College of Medicine

Massachusetts

Boston University School of Medicine

Michigan

Wayne State University School of Medicine

Missouri

Saint Louis University School of Medicine

University of Missouri—Kansas City School of Medicine

Nevada

University of Nevada

New Jersey

Rutgers University and Drexel University College of Medicine

Rutgers University and UMDNJ—New Jersey Medical School

Rutgers University and UMDNJ—Robert Wood Johnson Medical School

University of Medicine and Dentistry of New Jersey—New Jersey Medical School

New Mexico

University of New Mexico School of Medicine

New York

Brooklyn College and SUNY Downstate Medical Center

Hobart and William Smith Colleges/SUNY Upstate Medical University

Rensselaer Polytechnic Institute and Albany Medical College

St. Bonaventure University/The George Washington University School of Medicine and Health Sciences

Siena College and Albany Medical College

Sophie Davis School of Biomedical Education at the City College of New York

Stony Brook University and Stony Brook University School of Medicine

Union College and Albany Medical College

University of Rochester School of Medicine and Dentistry

Ohio

Case Western Reserve University School of Medicine

Northeastern Ohio Universities College of Medicine

University of Cincinnati College of Medicine

Pennsylvania

Drexel University and Drexel University College of Medicine

Lehigh University and Drexel University College of Medicine

Pennsylvania State University and Jefferson Medical College

Temple University School of Medicine

Villanova University and Drexel University College of Medicine

Wilkes University/SUNY-Upstate Medical University

Rhode Island

Warren Alpert Medical School of Brown University

Tennessee

Fisk University and Meharry Medical College

Texas

Rice University and Baylor College of Medicine

University of Texas School of Medicine at San Antonio

Virginia

Eastern Virginia Medical School

Virginia Commonwealth University School of Medicine

List of Medical Schools Offering Combined Undergraduate/M.D. Programs by Number of Years, 2014–15

6 Years

University of Missouri—Kansas City School of Medicine

6–7 Years

University of Miami

Northeastern Ohio Universities College of Medicine

Pennsylvania State University and Jefferson Medical College

7 Years

The George Washington University School of Medicine and Health Sciences and The Columbian School of Arts and Sciences

University of Florida College of Medicine

Northwestern University Feinberg School of Medicine

University of Illinois at Chicago College of Medicine

Boston University School of Medicine (8-year option available)

University of Medicine and Dentistry of New Jersey—

New Jersey Medical School

Rensselaer Polytechnic Institute and Albany Medical College

Sophie Davis School of Biomedical Education at the City College of New York

Drexel University and Drexel University College of Medicine

Lehigh University and Drexel University College of Medicine

Villanova University and Drexel University College of Medicine

Fisk University and Meharry Medical College

University of Texas School of Medicine at San Antonio

University of Nevada

8 Years

University of Alabama School of Medicine

University of South Alabama College of Medicine

University of California, San Diego School of Medicine

University of Connecticut and University of Connecticut School of Medicine

Howard University College of Medicine

University of New Mexico School of Medicine

Saint Louis University School of Medicine

Rutgers University and Drexel University College of Medicine

Rutgers University and UMDNJ—New Jersey Medical School

Rutgers University and UMDNJ—Robert Wood Johnson Medical School

Brooklyn College and SUNY Downstate Medical Center

Hobart and William Smith Colleges/SUNY Upstate Medical University

St. Bonaventure University/The George Washington University School of Medicine and Health Sciences

Siena College and Albany Medical College

Stony Brook University and Stony Brook University School of Medicine

Union College and Albany Medical College

University of Rochester School of Medicine and Dentistry

Case Western Reserve University School of Medicine

University of Cincinnati College of Medicine

Temple University School of Medicine

Wilkes University/SUNY-Upstate Medical University

Warren Alpert Medical School of Brown University

Rice University and Baylor College of Medicine

Eastern Virginia Medical School

Virginia Commonwealth University School of Medicine

Wayne State University School of Medicine

University of Southern California College of Letters, Arts, & Sciences and Keck School of Medicine

9 Years

University of Cincinnati College of Medicine
(College of Engineering—undergraduate)

CHAPTER 13:
M.D.–Ph.D. Dual Degree Programs

Interested in a career in research but are uncertain whether to pursue both an M.D. and a Ph.D.? Other options you can explore include:

- **Ph.D. in Biomedical Sciences** – You can earn a Ph.D. in biomedical sciences in graduate programs at medical schools. The program typically includes one or two years of core coursework, lab rotations to select a mentor, and three to four years of doctoral research. To learn more about available programs and how to apply, go to *www.aamc. org/phd.*

- **M.S. Degree or Certificate in Clinical Research** – You might also consider graduate work leading to a master's degree or certificate in clinical research. These programs, which can be pursued jointly or after receiving your Ph.D. or M.D. degree, are offered at many medical schools and graduate schools throughout the country.

- **"Year-Out" Program** – Another option is to take a year out from your M.D. program to conduct research under the direction of a mentor as part of a scholars program. Three such programs are the Fogarty International Clinical Research Scholarship Program, the NIH Medical Research Scholars Program, and the HHMI Research Fellows Program. See *www.fogartyscholars.org, www. cc.nih.gov/training/mrsp/index.html* and *www.hhmi.org/grants/individuals/ medical-fellows/* for details. In addition, many medical schools offer such opportunities for their students.

While many medical students plan to become full time practicing clinicians, there are other career paths that combine research, patient interaction, and teachings. A M.D.–Ph.D. Dual Degree Program, which provides training in both medicine and research prepares graduates to pursue a varied and engaging career.

The Education of a Physician-Scientist

Physician-scientists—those who are trained in both medicine and research—are greatly needed in today's world. There is a synergy that results when experimental and clinical thinking are joined, and that combination is found among those who have completed both M.D. and Ph.D. degrees. These individuals help translate the achievements of basic research into active clinical practice, and, in doing so, strengthen the link between medical knowledge and prevent, diagnose, and treat disease. If this is the path you prefer, you will enjoy a busy, challenging, and rewarding career.

Advantages of the M.D.-Ph.D. Dual Degree

One route to a career as a physician-scientist is enrollment in a combined M.D.-Ph.D. program. Although you can complete a Ph.D. program after receiving your M.D. degree, there are several advantages to pursuing joint M.D.-Ph.D. training:

- The greatest advantage of the dual-degree program is the integration of research and clinical training. This integrated approach may include seminars that cross departments and interactions with teams composed of both basic science and clinical investigators.

- In addition, you can save a significant amount of time. The combined program can be completed in a total of seven or eight years, compared to the nine or ten it would take to earn both degrees independently.

- Beyond that, M.D.-Ph.D. students enjoy opportunities for research and faculty mentoring frequently unavailable to M.D.-only students. As a result, these students are often able to enhance their mastery of the basic science background underlying patients' clinical problems, and, ultimately, use that information to develop improvements in diagnosis and treatment.

Research Specialties

Just as with a Ph.D.-only career, students with a combined degree can pursue many scientific specialties. Most students earn their Ph.D. degrees in biomedical laboratory disciplines such as biochemistry, biomedical engineering, biophysics, cell biology, genetics, immunology, microbiology, neuroscience, and pharmacology.

Explore M.D. – Ph.D. Programs

View a listing of M.D.-Ph.D. programs available at AAMC member medical schools at *www.aamc.org/students/research/mdphd/applying_md-phd/61570/mdphd_programs.html*

It is important to realize that not every research specialty is offered at every medical school, and that curricula can vary from institution to institution. In some schools, for example, M.D.-Ph.D. trainees also can complete their graduate work outside of laboratory disciplines in fields such as anthropology, computational biology, economics, engineering, health care policy, mathematics, physics, and sociology.

Clinical Specialties

M.D.-Ph.D. students can also pursue any one of many clinical specialties. The clinical specialty choices of students graduating from M.D.-Ph.D. programs over the past five years indicate that the most common residencies were internal medicine, pathology, and pediatrics.

When compared to M.D.-only graduates, M.D.-Ph.D. graduates have been more likely to enter residencies in radiation oncology, child neurology, and pathology and are less likely to go into family medicine, emergency medicine, and obstetrics/gynecology. Additionally, the majority of dual-degree students enter residencies after graduation. The approximately five percent that do not enter residency typically go straight into a postdoctoral fellowship position.

The Typical Program

Almost all U.S. and Canadian medical schools have M.D.-Ph.D. programs in one or more areas of specialization. Some are relatively small in size (one or two new students each year, with a dozen or so total students), while others are much larger (up to 25 new students annually and a total enrollment of around 190).

Although there are differences among programs, core elements are common to almost all. The typical program is completed in a total of seven to nine years and includes:

- Completion of the first two years of combined medical and graduate school coursework, followed by

- Three to five years of doctoral research, including the completion of a thesis project, and

- A return to medical school for core clinical training and electives during the final years of the medical curriculum.

At most schools, integrated approaches to graduate and medical education have been introduced throughout the curricula. In addition, most programs engage students in a wide range of other activities to enrich their training experience. The median time for completion of a M.D.-Ph.D. program is eight years.

Residency Programs after Graduation

Several residencies around the country offer highly structured programs in which research is fully integrated into clinical training. They differ in their overall composition but generally offer a shortened residency training period. For more information, visit *www.aamc.org/students/research/mdphd/career_paths/*.

Application and Admission

Nearly all M.D.-Ph.D. programs participate in the AMCAS® application process described in Chapter 6.

If you choose to pursue the dual-degree program, you will designate yourself as a Combined M.D.-Ph.D. Training Applicant and complete two additional essays—one related to why you are interested in the joint training program, and the other describing your research experience. Specifics in the application process—and the prerequisites required for admission—vary from school to school. (Some institutions, for example, require GRE scores.) For complete information, make certain to review the description of the dual-degree program at the web site of each medical school in which you are interested.

Factors Considered by the Admission Committee

Admission committee members will review the application materials for the usual experiences, attributes, and metrics that are important for admission of students to M.D.-only programs (see Chapter 7). But because M.D.-Ph.D. applicants plan to become both physicians and scientists, committee members will also look for evidence of an applicant's passion and aptitude for research. They accomplish this largely through review of an applicant's statement of career goals and in letters of evaluation from faculty or researchers with whom the applicant has previously worked. In particular, committee members seek confirmation of:

- Relevant and substantive research experience during or after college

- An appreciation for and understanding of the work of physician-scientists

- Intellectual drive, research ability, and perseverance

- Evidence of their passion and aptitude for research

If you hope to pursue the M.D.-Ph.D. joint degree, you will be expected to have clinical experience—be it through volunteer work, shadowing a physician-scientist, or specific training. Other experiences that admission committee members generally look favorably upon are similar to those of the M.D.-only candidate, such as leadership positions, community service activities, and teaching roles.

Finally, it's important to be aware that while significant weight is placed upon an applicant's interest and experience in research activities, he or she is also expected to demonstrate a degree of academic excellence similar to those accepted in the M.D.-only program. For students entering M.D.-Ph.D. programs in 2012, for example, the median GPA for students was 3.8 and total MCAT® scores was 34.5* as reported by the American Medical College Application Service (AMCAS).

Keep in mind that the range of GPAs and MCAT® scores for accepted applicants is quite broad, and considered in conjunction with other selection factors.

Lisiting of Policies by M.D.-Ph.D. Program

Review policies of M.D.-Ph.D. programs at *www.aamc.org/mdphd/faqtable.pdf*.

Medical Scientist Training Program (MSTP)

The MSTP currently has 44 participating programs with a total of 932 trainees. About 170 positions for new students are available nationwide each year. For more information, see *www.nigms.nih.gov/Training/InstPredoc/PredocOverview-MSTP.htm*.

Acceptance Policies

Just as application requirements vary from school to school, so too do their acceptance policies. Some institutions permit an applicant who is not accepted to the M.D.-Ph.D. dual degree program to pursue admission to the M.D.-only curriculum. Other medical schools will accept applications from M.D.-Ph.D. candidates only for both degree programs, and failure to gain admittance to one program precludes consideration from another. Since school policies differ, applicants should clarify these matters at each school prior to application, and let admission office staff know of their interest in pursuing an M.D.-only program (if that is the case) should they not be admitted to the dual-degree program.

Financing M.D. – Ph.D. Programs

The sources of funding for M.D.-Ph.D. programs vary from school to school. Many schools offer full support for both the M.D. and Ph.D. components of their education, including tuition waivers, a stipend, and health insurance. At other institutions, varying degrees of support are available, sometimes only for the Ph.D. component of the program. Before you apply to an M.D.-Ph.D. dual-degree program, you should determine the level of financial assistance available.

A significant amount of funding comes from institutional sources and both individual and institutional grants. The latter includes the Medical Scientist Training Program (MSTP) sponsored by the National Institutes of Health (NIH), as well as other NIH grants. While you will undoubtedly want to review the list of medical schools participating in the MSTP (*www.nigms.nih.gov/Training/InstPredoc/PredocInst-MSTP.htm*), you will also want to contact the program officials at the institu-tions of interest and review their web sites for full information.

Bear in mind that although most M.D.-Ph.D. programs offer support for their students, additional resources are available. Most take the form of competitive applications submitted by the trainee and their research mentor. These include fellowships from both private sources and a number of NIH institutes. You can review the list of these opportunities at *www.aamc.org/mdphd/fundingformdphd.pdf*.

For additional information and guidance about application to and enrollment in a combined M.D.-Ph.D. program, please visit the AAMC's web site on the dual-degree program at www.aamc.org/mdphd or contact your pre-health advisor and the M.D.-Ph.D. program director at the medical schools of interest.

For additional information regarding clinical specialties, see:

Brass LF, Akabas MH, Burnley LD, Engman DM, Wiley CA, Andersen OS. Are MD-PhD programs meeting their goals? An analysis of career choices made by graduates of 24 M.D.-Ph.D. programs. Acad Med. 2010; 85(4):692-701.

Paik JC, Howard G, Lorenz RG. Postgraduate choices of graduates from medical scientist training programs, 2004-2008. JAMA. 2009; 302(12):1271-3.

CHAPTER 14:
Information About U.S. Medical Schools
Accredited by the LCME

MSAR® Online – Complete U.S. Medical School Profiles

For complete, detailed information on each United States medical school, including MCAT and GPA data, school-specific admission requirements and policies, applicant and acceptee statistics, and side-by-side medical school comparisons, purchase the MSAR® Online. For more information about MSAR® Online, a preview of the site and complete list of site features, data, and information, visit *www.aamc.org/msar*.

U.S. Medical Schools

Alabama

University of Alabama School of Medicine

University of South Alabama
College of Medicine

Arizona

University of Arizona College of Medicine - Phoenix

University of Arizona College of Medicine - Tucson

Arkansas

University of Arkansas College of Medicine

California

Keck School of Medicine of the
University of Southern California

Loma Linda University School of Medicine

Stanford University School of Medicine

University of California, Davis,
School of Medicine

University of California, Irvine
School of Medicine

University of California, Los Angeles
David Geffen School of Medicine at UCLA

University of California, Riverside,
School of Medicine

University of California, San Diego,
School of Medicine

University of California, San Francisco,
School of Medicine

Colorado

University of Colorado School of Medicine

Connecticut

Frank H. Netter MD School of Medicine at
Quinnipiac University

University of Connecticut
School of Medicine

Yale University School of Medicine

District of Columbia

The George Washington University
School of Medicine and Health Sciences

Georgetown University School of Medicine

Howard University College of Medicine

Florida

Florida Atlantic University Charles E. Schmidt
College of Medicine

Florida International University
Herbert Wertheim College of Medicine

Florida State University
College of Medicine

University of Central Florida
College of Medicine

University of Florida College of Medicine

University of Miami Miller
School of Medicine

University of South Florida
Morsani College of Medicine

Georgia

Emory University School of Medicine

Medical College of Georgia at Georgia Regents University

Mercer University School of Medicine

Morehouse School of Medicine

Hawaii

University of Hawaii John A. Burns School of Medicine

Illinois

Loyola University Chicago Stritch School of Medicine

Northwestern University The Feinberg School of Medicine

Rosalind Franklin University of Medicine and Science Chicago Medical School

Rush Medical College of Rush University

Southern Illinois University School of Medicine

University of Chicago Division of the Biological Sciences, The Pritzker School of Medicine

University of Illinois at Chicago College of Medicine

Indiana

Indiana University School of Medicine

Iowa

University of Iowa Roy J. and Lucille A. Carver College of Medicine

Kansas

University of Kansas School of Medicine

Kentucky

University of Kentucky College of Medicine

University of Louisville School of Medicine

Louisiana

Louisiana State University School of Medicine in New Orleans

Louisiana State University Health Sciences Center School of Medicine in Shreveport

Tulane University School of Medicine

Maryland

Johns Hopkins University School of Medicine

Uniformed Services University of the Health Sciences F. Edward Hébert School of Medicine

University of Maryland School of Medicine

Massachusetts

Boston University School of Medicine

Harvard Medical School

Tufts University School of Medicine

University of Massachusetts Medical School

Michigan

Central Michigan University College of Medicine

Michigan State University College of Human Medicine

Oakland University William Beaumont School of Medicine

University of Michigan Medical School

Wayne State University School of Medicine

Western Michigan University School of Medicine

Minnesota

Mayo Medical School

University of Minnesota Medical School

Mississippi

University of Mississippi School of Medicine

Missouri

Saint Louis University School of Medicine

University of Missouri Columbia School of Medicine

University of Missouri — Kansas City School of Medicine

Washington University School of Medicine

Nebraska

Creighton University School of Medicine

University of Nebraska College of Medicine

Nevada

University of Nevada School of Medicine

New Hampshire

Geisel School of Medicine at Dartmouth

New Jersey

Cooper Medical School of Rowan University

University of Medicine and Dentistry of New Jersey — New Jersey Medical School

University of Medicine and Dentistry of New Jersey — Robert Wood Johnson Medical School

New Mexico

University of New Mexico School of Medicine

New York

Albany Medical College

Albert Einstein College of Medicine of Yeshiva University

Columbia University College of Physicians and Surgeons

Hofstra North Shore — LIJ School of Medicine at Hofstra University

Icahn School of Medicine at Mount Sinai

New York Medical College

New York University School of Medicine

State University of New York Downstate Medical Center College of Medicine

State University of New York Upstate Medical Center College of Medicine

Stony Brook University School of Medicine

University at Buffalo School of Medicine and Biomedical Sciences

University of Rochester School of Medicine and Dentistry

Weill Cornell Medical College

North Carolina

The Brody School of Medicine at East Carolina University

Duke University School of Medicine

University of North Carolina at Chapel Hill School of Medicine

Wake Forest University School of Medicine of Wake Forest Baptist Medical Center

North Dakota

University of North Dakota School of Medicine and Health Sciences

Ohio

Case Western Reserve University School of Medicine

Northeastern Ohio Medical University

The Ohio State University College of Medicine

University of Cincinnati College of Medicine

The University of Toledo College of Medicine

Wright State University Boonshoft School of Medicine

Oklahoma

University of Oklahoma College of Medicine

Oregon

Oregon Health & Science University School of Medicine

Pennsylvania

The Commonwealth Medical College

Drexel University College of Medicine

Jefferson Medical College of Thomas Jefferson University

Pennsylvania State University College of Medicine

Raymond and Ruth Perelman School of Medicine at the University of Pennsylvania

Temple University School of Medicine

University of Pittsburgh School of Medicine

Puerto Rico

Ponce School of Medicine

San Juan Bautista School of Medicine

Universidad Central del Caribe School of Medicine

University of Puerto Rico School of Medicine

Rhode Island

The Warren Alpert Medical School of Brown University

South Carolina

Medical University of South Carolina College of Medicine

University of South Carolina School of Medicine

University of South Carolina School of Medicine—Greenville

South Dakota

University of South Dakota Sanford
School of Medicine

Tennessee

East Tennessee State University

James H. Quillen College of Medicine

Meharry Medical College
School of Medicine

University of Tennessee Health Science
Center College of Medicine

Vanderbilt University School of Medicine

Texas

Baylor College of Medicine

Texas Tech University Health Sciences
Center at El Paso — Paul L. Foster School of
Medicine

Texas A&M University System Health Science
Center College of Medicine

Texas Tech University Health Sciences Center
School of Medicine

University of Texas Medical Branch at
Galveston

University of Texas Medical
School at Houston

University of Texas
School of Medicine at San Antonio

University of Texas Southwestern
Medical Center at Dallas Southwestern
Medical School

Utah

University of Utah School of Medicine

Vermont

University of Vermont College of Medicine

Virginia

Eastern Virginia Medical School

University of Virginia School of Medicine

Virginia Commonwealth University
School of Medicine

Virginia Tech Carilion School of Medicine

Washington

University of Washington
School of Medicine

West Virginia

Marshall University Joan C. Edwards
School of Medicine

West Virginia University School of Medicine

Wisconsin

Medical College of Wisconsin

University of Wisconsin
School of Medicine and Public Health

CHAPTER 15:

Information About Canadian Medical Schools
Accredited by the LCME and by the CACMS

The 17 medical schools in Canada are members of the Association of Faculties of Medicine of Canada (www.afmc.ca) and affiliate members of the AAMC. They participate in the activities of both associations. Canadian medical schools are accredited jointly by the Liaison Committee on Medical Education (www.lcme.org, LCME) and the Committee on Accreditation of Canadian Medical Schools (www.afmc.ca/index-e.php, CACMS). All are M.D. degree granting schools with high-quality educational programs.

Admission policies and procedures of Canadian schools are similar in many respects to those followed in U.S. schools; thus, many of the suggestions for applicants in chapters 1 through 9 will also apply. Schools vary with respect to the emphasis placed on selection factors, and applicants are encouraged to refer to the individual school entries for additional details.

Fifteen Canadian medical schools offer four-year educational programs; two, McMaster and Calgary, are three-year programs. Some students at the Université de Montréal are admitted into a one-year preparatory program prior to beginning the M.D. curriculum. McGill University's five-year M.D. program includes an initial year that must be completed by graduates of the province of Quebec's Collège d'enseignement général et professionnel (CÉGEP).

Table 15-A

Subjects Required by Two or More Canadian Medical Schools, 2012–2013 Entering Class

Required Subject	# of Schools
Biochemistry	6
Biology	7
Calculus	2
College English	4
College Mathematics	2
Humanities	3
Inorganic Chemistry	7
Organic Chemistry	8
Physics	6
Social Sciences	2

NOTE: n=17. Figures based on data provided fall 2012. Four of the 17 medical schools (Dalhousie, Northern Ontario, McMaster, and Western Ontario) did not indicate specific course requirements and are not included in the tabulations.

Selection Criteria

Canadian medical schools vary with respect to the number of years of undergraduate instruction required of applicants. Medical schools also vary with respect to recommended content during premedical undergraduate education. Table 15-A shows that physics, inorganic and organic chemistry, biology, biochemistry, humanities, and English are the most common subjects required in undergraduate education by the Canadian medical schools.

Language of Instruction

Three Canadian medical schools—Laval, Montréal and Sherbrooke, all located in the province of Quebec—require students to be fluent in French as all instruction is in that language. Instruction in the other 14 schools is in English, and the University of Ottawa offers the M.D. curriculum in both French and English.

In Canada, universities fall under provincial jurisdiction and the majority of places in each faculty of medicine are allocated to permanent residents of the province in which the university is located.

Not all faculties of medicine accept applications from international students. Conversely, some faculties of medicine may reserve positions for international students, possibly as part of agreements with foreign governments and institutions. Statistics compiled by the Association of Faculties of Medicine of Canada (www.afmc.ca) show that most medical schools admit international students. In 2011-2012, 141 U.S. students applied to the 11

Table 15-B

Tuition and Student Fees for 2012–2013 First-Year Students at Canadian Medical Schools (in Canadian Dollars)

Categories of Students	Range	Average
In-Province	$4,171-$24,704	$14,613*
Canada, Out-of-Province	$7,424-$24,704	$16,118*
Visa	$17,141-$57,828	$32,330*

NOTE: Figures based on data provided fall 2012

* Average In-Province data were derived from all 17 Canadian schools. Average Out-of-Province data were derived from all 17 Canadian schools reporting. Average visa data were derived from 7 schools that accept foreign students.

Source: Association of Faculties of Medicine of Canada

Canadian medical schools that supplied data and recorded a 5.7 percent success rate. In the same year, 187 non-U.S. international students applied to the 11 Canadian medical schools that supplied data and recorded a 5.3 percent success rate. The success rate for Canadian applicants to the same schools was 25.2 percent. Additional information about Canadian medical schools can be found in the Association of Faculties of Medicine of Canada publication, Admission Requirements of Canadian Faculties of Medicine (2013) www.afmc.ca/publications-admission-e.php.

Positions filled by international students in Canadian medical schools are not necessarily subsidized by provincial/territorial governments. As such, international students, including U.S. students, may pay higher tuition and fees compared to those of Canadian residents.

Academic Record/Suitability

Although an excellent academic record is a very important factor in gaining admission to a Canadian medical school, great deal of effort is expended in assessing applicants' suitability for a medical career based on other factors. Personal suitability is assessed in a variety of ways by the schools; applicants who can demonstrate that they possess the qualities considered important in the practice of medicine may sometimes be admitted even if their academic record is not outstanding. Alternately, applicants with outstanding records who do not possess these qualities may not gain a place in medical school.

Most applicants to Canadian medical schools are interviewed prior to acceptance, so the interview information in Chapter 7 will be useful.

Medical College Admission Test (MCAT®)

Eleven Canadian medical schools require applicants to take the MCAT®: Alberta, British Columbia, Calgary, Dalhousie, Manitoba, McMaster, Memorial, Queen's, Saskatchewan, Toronto, and Western Ontario.

Other Considerations

Canadian faculties of medicine do not discriminate on the basis of race, religion, or gender in admitting new students. The admission of Aboriginal students (First Nations, Inuit, Métis) is encouraged at Canadian medical schools and most allocate positions specifically for Aboriginal applicants including Laval, Sherbrooke, Montréal, McGill, Ottawa, Queen's, McMaster, Western Ontario, Northern Ontario School of Medicine, Saskatchewan, Alberta, and British Columbia.

The number of female applicants has leveled off in recent years, with correspondingly consistent proportions of women in schools' entering classes. Women comprised 54 percent of the 2011–2012 applicant pool, and the success rate for women was slightly higher than that for men. The 2012 entering classes at the 11 Canadian medical schools reporting data about male and female matriculants included 55 percent women and 45 percent men. Overall, 25 percent of applicants received at least one offer of admission.

Expenses/Financial Aid

Tuition and student fees for Canadian and non-Canadian students in the 2012 entering class are provided in Table 15-B and in individual school entries. Expenses vary from school to school and from student to student. Tuition at several Canadian schools is slightly higher for the first year than for successive years. Some financial aid information is provided in the individual school entries. Eligible Canadian students may apply for a Canadian Student Loan, or they may apply to the Department of Education in their province for a provincial student loan.

Canadian Medical Schools

Alberta

University of Alberta Faculty of Medicine and Dentistry

University of Calgary Faculty of Medicine

British Columbia

University of British Columbia Faculty of Medicine

Manitoba

University of Manitoba Faculty of Medicine

Newfoundland

Memorial University of Newfoundland Faculty of Medicine

Nova Scotia

Dalhousie University Faculty of Medicine

Ontario

McMaster University, Michael G. DeGroote School of Medicine

Queen's University Faculty of Health Sciences

University of Ottawa Faculty of Medicine

University of Toronto Faculty of Medicine

Northern Ontario School of Medicine

Western University—Schulich School of Medicine & Dentistry

Quebec

Université Laval Faculty of Medicine

McGill University Faculty of Medicine

Université de Montréal Faculty of Medicine

Université de Sherbrooke Faculty of Medicine

Saskatchewan

University of Saskatchewan College of Medicine

MSAR® Online – Complete Medical School Profiles

For detailed information on each Canadian medical school, including MCAT and GPA data, school-specific admission requirements and policies, applicant and acceptee statistics, and side-by-side medical school comparisons, purchase the MSAR® Online. For more information about MSAR® Online, a preview of the site and complete list of site features, data, and information, visit *www.aamc.org/msar*.

Resources and Publications

Resources for Other Health Careers

1. **American Academy of Physician Assistants**
   2318 Mill Road, Alexandria, VA 22332
   (703) 836-2272
   www.aapa.org

2. **American Association of Colleges of Osteopathic Medicine**
   5550 Friendship Boulevard, Suite 310
   Chevy Chase, MD 20815-7231
   (301) 968-4100
   www.aacom.org

3. **American Association of Colleges of Pharmacy**
   1727 King Street
   Alexandria, VA 22314-2815
   (703) 739-2330
   www.aacp.org

4. **American Association of Colleges of Podiatric Medicine**
   15850 Crabbs Branch Way, Suite 320
   Rockville, MD 20855-4307
   (301) 948-9760
   info@aacpm.org; www.aacpm.org

5. **American Association of Colleges of Nursing**
   One Dupont Circle, N.W., Suite 530
   Washington, D.C. 20036
   (202) 463-6930
   www.aacn.nche.edu

6. **American Association of Dental Schools**
   1400 K Street, N.W., Suite 1100
   Washington, D.C. 20005
   (202) 289-7201
   www.adea.org

7. **Association of American Veterinary Medical Colleges**
   1101 Vermont Avenue, N.W., Suite 301
   Washington, D.C. 20005-3521
   (202) 371-9195
   www.aavmc.org

8. **Association of Schools and Colleges of Optometry**
   6110 Executive Boulevard, Suite 420
   Rockville, MD 20852
   (301) 231-5944
   www.opted.org

9. **Association of Schools of Public Health**
   1900 M Street NW, Suite 710
   Washington, DC 20036
   (202) 296-1099
   info@asph.org; www.asph.org

10. **ExploreHealthCareers.org**
    American Dental Education Association
    1400 K Street, NW, Suite 1100
    Washington, DC 20005
    (202) 289-7201; (347) 365-9253

Publications for the Health Professions

1. **Autsin, L.,** *What's Holding You Back? 8 Critical Choices for Women's Success*
   $14.00
   Basic Books, 2000
   www.perseusbooksgroup.com/basic/book_detail.jsp?isbn=046503263X

2. **Bickel, J.,** *Women in Medicine: Getting In, Growing & Advancing*
   $48.00
   Sage, 2000
   1-800-818-7243
   www.sagepub.com/books/Book9436?

3. *Educational Survival Skills Study Guide*
   Free
   Office of Statewide Health Planning and Development
   Health Professions Career Opportunity Program
   400 R Street, Suite 330
   Sacramento, CA 95811-6213
   www.oshpd.ca.gov/

4. *Financial Advice and Health Careers Resources Directory for Students*
   Free
   Office of Statewide Health Planning and Development
   Health Professions Careers Opportunity Program
   400 R Street, Suite 330
   Sacramento, CA 95811-6213

5. *The Journal for Minority Medical Students*
   Free, published quarterly
   Spectrum Unlimited
   1194A Buckhead Crossing
   Woodstock, GA 30189
   (770) 852-2671
   http://issuu.com/journalforminoritymedstudents/docs/magazine

6. **Kaltreider, Nancy B.,** *Dilemmas of a Double Life, Women Balancing Careers and Relationship*
   $49.95
   Jason Aronson, Inc., 1997
   (800) 462-6420

7. *Minorities in Medicine: A Guide for Premedical Students*
   Free
   Office of Statewide Health Planning and Development
   Health Professions Career Opportunity Program
   400 R Street, Suite 330
   Sacramento, CA 95811-6213

8. **More, E.S.,** *Restoring the Balance: Women Physicians and the Profession of Medicine, 1850–1995.*
   $37.50 paperback
   Harvard University Press, 2000
   www.amazon.com/Restoring-Balance-Physicians-Profession-1850-1995/dp/0674005678

9. *Need a Lift? College Financial Aid Handbook*
   $1.95, available on CD-Rom
   The American Legion
   P.O. Box 36460
   Indianapolis, IN 46236
   (888) 453-4466
   http://pdf.needalift.org/NAL2009.pdf

10. *The Student Guide*
    U.S. Department of Education Federal Student Aid Information Center
    P.O. Box 84
    Washington, D.C. 20044-0084
    (800) 4-FED-AID, (800) 433-3243
    http://studentaid.ed.gov/students/attachments/siteresources/12-13_Guide.pdf

11. *Time Management for Students*
    Free
    Office of Statewide Health Planning and Development
    Health Professions Career Opportunity Program
    400 R Street, Suite 330
    Sacramento, CA 95811-6213

12. **Wear, D. (Ed),** *Women in Medical Education: An Anthology of Experience*
    $52.50 hardcover, $29.95 paperback
    SUNY Press, 1996
    www.sunypress.edu/p-2424-women-in-medical-education.aspx

13. *The Young Scientist: A Career Guide for Underrepresented Science Graduates*
    Free, published annually
    Spectrum Unlimited
    1194A Buckhead Crossing
    Woodstock, GA 30189
    (770) 852-2671, (504) 433-5040
    http://issuu.com/journalforminoritymedstudents/docs/youngscientist2009

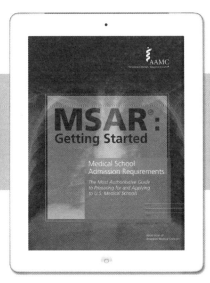
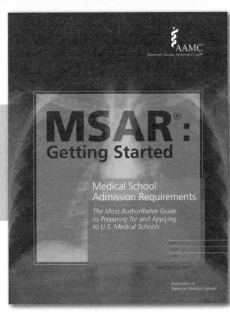

Tomorrow's Doctors, Tomorrow's Cures®

FIRST

Financial **I**nformation, **R**esources, **S**ervices, and **T**ools

Empowering students to borrow wisely and repay responsibly.

Calculate your monthly payment
Medloans® Organizer and Calculator

Set up your budget
Financial Literacy 101

www.aamc.org/first

Find the right resources
FIRST's Financial Aid Toolkit

Student Loans	Interest Rate		Years to Repay
	6.8%	+	10

My Finances			
Perkins Loan	$5,000	5.000%	10yrs
Grad PLUS	$47,000	7.900%	10yrs

Association of
American Medical Colleges

Official MCAT® Preparation

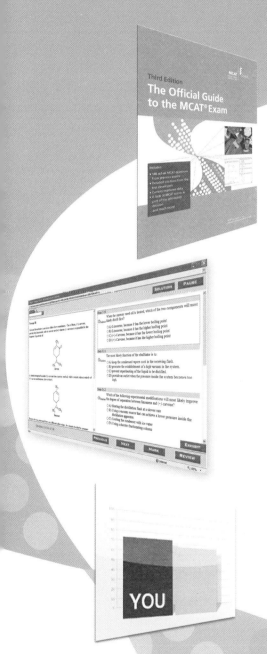

Step 1: Learn the basics
The Official Guide to the MCAT® Exam
Full of tips and data to help you plan,
along with 146 unique test items with solutions.
www.aamc.org/officialmcatguide

Step 2: Get a baseline score
Free MCAT Practice Test 3
Take a timed test to learn how you might
perform on the actual exam.
www.e-mcat.com

Step 3: Analyze your MCAT knowledge
The Official MCAT® Self-Assessment Package
Buy a self-assessment to learn your strengths and weaknesses
to target during study.
www.aamc.org/mcatsap

Step 4: Study & track progress
Seven additional practice tests
Take more timed tests to track improvements
and to study with real test items.
www.e-mcat.com

MCAT® is a program of the
Association of American Medical Colleges

⚕ ASPIRING DOCS

Inspiration and resources so anyone can aspire to be a physician

Is a career in medicine right for me?

How do I apply?

How do I shadow a doctor?

How do I pay for med school?

What's it like to take the MCAT?

 www.facebook.com/aspiringdocs

 www.twitter.com/Aspiring_Docs

 www.aspiringdocsdiaries.org

 www.aamc.org/aspiringdocs

Association of
American Medical Colleges